MW00827640

# The Economic Status of the Hispanic Population

## Selected Essays

A volume in
*The Hispanic Population in the United States*
Richard R. Verdugo, *Series Editor*

# The Economic Status of the Hispanic Population

## Selected Essays

*edited by*

## Marie T. Mora
*The University of Texas–Pan American*

## Alberto Dávila
*The University of Texas–Pan American*

INFORMATION AGE PUBLISHING, INC.
Charlotte, NC • www.infoagepub.com

**Library of Congress Cataloging-in-Publication Data**

A CIP record for this book is available from the Library of Congress
  http://www.loc.gov

Copyright © 2013 Information Age Publishing Inc.

All rights reserved. No part of this publication may be reproduced, stored in a
retrieval system, or transmitted, in any form or by any means, electronic, mechanical,
photocopying, microfilming, recording or otherwise, without written permission
from the publisher.

Printed in the United States of America

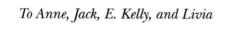

*To Anne, Jack, E. Kelly, and Livia*

# CONTENTS

# PREFACE

One of the major demographic shifts in the United States in the last three decades has been the rapid growth in the Hispanic population. Indeed, the number of Hispanic Americans in the 50 states and the District of Columbia has more than tripled since 1980 (rising from 14.6 million to 50.5 million 30 years later), such that they currently represent one of every six people in the country. This striking demographic change means that understanding and monitoring factors related to the economic status of Hispanics has become increasingly important for the economic conditions in the United States overall.[1]

Recognizing the escalating importance of this demographic group, sociologist Richard Verdugo proposed a series of volumes to *Information Age Publishing* that would explore a variety of socioeconomic and demographic outcomes of Hispanic Americans, including one that would focus on their economic status—the purpose of this particular volume. Others in the series analyze issues related to education, labor market outcomes, social issues, political and civic engagement, and demographic implications of the growing Hispanic population. In 2009, Richard invited us to be the editors of this volume, an invitation we were excited to accept. At the time, the Great Recession (which officially started in December 2007 and ended in June 2009) was still underway, which emphasized the need to better understand economic conditions affecting large segments of the U.S. population.

One undercurrent throughout this volume is that Hispanics tend to lag behind non-Hispanics with respect to a variety of economic-status measures, including educational attainment, English-language fluency (due to the relatively high share of immigrants among Hispanics), earnings, asset

*The Economic Status of the Hispanic Population,* pages ix–xii
Copyright © 2013 by Information Age Publishing
All rights of reproduction in any form reserved.

accumulation and income, and access to health care, among others. Despite lagging behind, however, some of the chapters show that Hispanics appear to have made some progress with respect to narrowing these gaps vis-à-vis non-Hispanics in the first decade of the millennium. Moreover, it is clear that many of these outcomes overlap. Not surprisingly, workers with low levels of education (or who have difficulty in communicating) often have a hard time finding jobs that pay well and offer generous benefits (like health insurance). The relatively low education levels of Hispanics as a group, therefore, explain some of their other relatively low economic outcomes. Consequently, one issue that many of the chapters explore is the extent to which Hispanic/non-Hispanic differences in economic-status measures can be explained by differences in their socioeconomic and demographic characteristics, such as education.

One difficulty we encountered while working on this volume was how to assess "economic status". Clearly a variety of measures exist, and an entire volume could have been devoted to investigating one specific measure. We therefore realize that the chapters presented here do not cover every economic outcome that readers might want to see. When we invited the various authors to participate in this project, we did not direct them to write about a specific topic; instead we wanted to provide them with a forum to discuss Hispanic economic issues that they felt deserved more attention.

The authors were instructed, however, to present their research in an interesting and "reader-friendly" manner. The intended audience is much broader than one comprised of quantitatively oriented academics in the social sciences; it also includes students, policymakers, and anyone interested in learning more about the economic conditions of Hispanic Americans. As such, while most of the chapters employ rigorous statistical methods, to prevent readers from getting bogged down (or bored!) with the empirical details and technical jargon, these details have been placed in footnotes or chapter appendices. Of course, readers desiring to learn more about these details should feel free to contact the chapters' authors.

Readers will notice that some chapters employ the term "Hispanic" while others use "Latino". As both terms are often used interchangeably, we decided to let each author use the term he/she preferred. Both of the terms have flaws, however, as they sometimes provide the illusion of a homogeneous demographic group. As several of the chapters point out (including ours), the Hispanic/Latino population is quite diverse along a variety of demographic dimensions (such as immigration, reasons for migration, culture, and so forth). This heterogeneity adds to the challenge of editing a volume like this one; the economic experience of "Hispanics" as a group could be rather different for specific subgroups within the Hispanic population. This fact is often overlooked in the literature and by policymakers.

The order of the chapters in this volume was based on identifying three general themes in the chapters we received. The first three chapters focus on education-related issues. In Chapter one, in addition to providing an overview of various economic outcomes of Hispanics versus non-Hispanics in the United States (including their labor market earnings, homeownership rates, the propensity to earn interest or dividend income, and health insurance coverage), we estimate the role that education (and other socioeconomic and demographic characteristics) plays in explaining these outcomes. Mark Hugo López in Chapter two discusses differences in educational aspirations and attainment between Hispanics and other youths. Arturo Gonzalez in the third chapter explores a more nuanced outcome of U.S. schooling: literacy in the English language; he uses this outcome as a measure of assimilation of different generations of Hispanic immigrants into U.S. society.

The next three chapters provide insight into poverty and inequality issues among Hispanics. In Chapter four, Mary Lopez discusses differences in poverty rates across several demographic dimensions, including race/ethnicity, gender, and nativity; she also analyzes how various socioeconomic and demographic factors (such as education, employment, and marital status) contribute to the probability of residing in poverty for Hispanics and non-Hispanics Whites. Continuing with the poverty theme, Carlos Siordia and Ruben Farias in Chapter five consider whether the geographic concentration of Hispanics differently affects the likelihood of being impoverished between Hispanics and non-Hispanic Whites. Refugio Rochin in Chapter six adds to this discussion by providing an overview of how changes in the concentration of Hispanics in rural areas have affected these areas' socioeconomic outcomes.

Chapters seven through nine pertain to health-related behaviors and outcomes as well as time-use patterns among Hispanics. In Chapter seven, Jillian Medeiros and Gabriel Sanchez discuss possible reasons why the health insurance coverage rates among Hispanics are relatively low; they further analyze how the cost of medical care affected the economic standing (such as having to borrow to pay medical bills) and health-related behavior (such as seeking medical attention when needed) among Hispanic registered voters during the Great Recession. Veronica Salinas, Jillian Medeiros, and Melissa Binder in the following chapter investigate how differences in socioeconomic and demographic characteristics, including education and time-use (e.g., exercising vs. being sedentary), relate to two specific health outcomes—body mass index and the incidence of obesity—between Hispanics and non-Hispanic Whites. In Chapter nine, Andres Vargas studies differences in time-use patterns (such as the time spent working or exercising) between married Hispanic immigrants and U.S.-born non-Hispanic Whites.

In the final chapter, we discuss some of the lessons learned from the other chapters regarding Hispanic economic outcomes; we also raise several questions worthy of future research. Providing insight into such questions will become increasingly valuable to the economic status of the nation overall because as the Hispanic population continues to grow, it will play an even larger role than now in determining the economic direction of the United States.

## NOTE

1. It should be noted that this volume focuses on Hispanics in the 50 states and the District of Columbia. An entire volume could have been devoted to analyzing Hispanic economic outcomes in Puerto Rico and other U.S. territories.

# ACKNOWLEDGEMENTS

We express our appreciation to all of the contributors to this volume for the enthusiastic effort they put into their chapters as well as their patience throughout the process. We particularly want to thank Richard R. Verdugo for inviting us to undertake this project, which is part of an exciting series on *The Hispanic Population in the United States*. Finally, we acknowledge the work of Ms. Xu Sun, who helped with many of the formatting and technical details for this volume during the Summer of 2012.

*The Economic Status of the Hispanic Population*, page xiii
Copyright © 2013 by Information Age Publishing
All rights of reproduction in any form reserved.

# LIST OF CONTRIBUTORS

**Melissa Binder, Ph.D.**
Associate Professor of Economics
Department of Economics
University of New Mexico
Albuquerque, New Mexico

**Alberto Dávila, Ph.D.**
Professor of Economics and V. F. "Doc"
    and Gertrude M. Chair
    for Entrepreneurship
Department of Economics
    and Finance
The University of Texas–Pan American
Edinburg, Texas

**Ruben Antonio Farias, M.S.**
Graduate Student of Sociology
Department of Sociology
Texas A&M University
College Station, Texas

**Arturo Gonzalez, Ph.D.**
Financial Economist
Office of the Comptroller of the Currency
Washington, District of Columbia

**Mark Hugo López, Ph.D.**
Associate Director
Pew Hispanic Center
Washington, District of Columbia

**Mary J. Lopez, Ph.D.**
Associate Professor of Economics
Department of Economics
Occidental College
Los Angeles, California

**Jillian Medeiros, Ph.D.**
Assistant Professor of Political Science
Department of Political Science
University of New Mexico
Albuquerque, New Mexico

**Marie T. Mora, Ph.D.**
Professor of Economics
Department of Economics
    and Finance
The University of Texas–Pan American
Edinburg, Texas

*The Economic Status of the Hispanic Population,* pages xv–xvi
Copyright © 2013 by Information Age Publishing
All rights of reproduction in any form reserved.

**Refugio I. Rochin, Ph.D.**
Professor Emeritus of Chicana/o
    Studies and Agricultural Economics
    University of California, Davis; and
Director Emeritus for Research and
    Evaluation in Education
University of California, Santa Cruz,
    California

**Veronica Salinas, M.A.**
Ph.D. Candidate in Economics
Department of Economics
University of New Mexico
Albuquerque, New Mexico

**Gabriel Sanchez, Ph.D.**
Associate Professor of Political Science
Department of Political Science
University of New Mexico
Albuquerque, New Mexico

**Carlos Siordia, Ph.D.**
Assistant Research Professor
Preventive Medicine and Community
    Health
University of Texas Medical Branch
Galveston, Texas

**Andres J. Vargas, Ph.D.**
Assistant Professor of Economics
Department of Economics
Texas Tech University
Lubbock, Texas

CHAPTER 1

# AN OVERVIEW OF HISPANIC ECONOMIC OUTCOMES IN THE FIRST DECADE OF THE 2000s

**Marie T. Mora**
*The University of Texas–Pan American*

**Alberto Dávila**
*The University of Texas–Pan American*

Hispanic population growth, in both relative and absolute terms, represents one of the striking demographic changes in the United States during the first decade of the new millennium. Between 2000 and 2010, the number of Hispanics in the country rose by 45%, from 35.3 million (one out of every eight people) to 50.5 million (one out of every six), outstripping the 4.9% increase in the non-Hispanic population. Indeed, as reported in a 2011 Pew Hispanic Center report by Jeffrey Passel, D'Vera Cohn, and Mark Hugo López, Hispanics drove more than half of the entire U.S. population growth in the decade. Immigration as well as relatively high fertility rates explain these changes.

*The Economic Status of the Hispanic Population*, pages 1–21
Copyright © 2013 by Information Age Publishing
All rights of reproduction in any form reserved.

These demographic shifts indicate that the economic status of Hispanics has become increasingly important for the welfare of the nation as a whole. On the one hand, the dramatic growth in the Hispanic population has positive implications with respect to certain economic outcomes. For example, Hispanics as a group are relatively young, and they tend to have a relatively strong attachment to the labor force (particularly men). These demographics offset some of the retirement implications of the baby boomers. The purchasing power of Hispanics has also been rising dramatically—doubling by some estimates to $1 trillion—between 2000 and 2010 (e.g., Selig Center for Economic Growth, 2010), a pace that outstripped their overall population growth.

On the other hand, Hispanics have less education on average than non-Hispanics, dampening their income and asset accumulation potential. Indeed, as we show in this chapter, the earnings and other economic status measures of Hispanics, including their homeownership rates, the likelihood of earning interest and dividend income, and health insurance coverage, are considerably lower than those of non-Hispanics. A closer examination of the data, however, reveals that the bulk of these disparities can be explained by differences in education and other observable demographic and socioeconomic characteristics between the populations. Moreover, despite lagging behind non-Hispanics, Hispanics appeared to gain some ground with respect to their educational attainment and other socioeconomic outcomes in the first decade of the 2000s.

## THE GROWING HISPANIC PRESENCE IN THE TRADITIONAL WORKING-AGE POPULATION

The top panel in Figure 1.1 illustrates the rising share of Hispanics among adults ages 25–64 (the traditional working ages) in the United States during the first decade of the twenty-first century.[1] Note that in every year between 2000 and 2010, the representation of Hispanics increased, such that their share of 14.9% among adults in 2010 was one and a third times higher than their 11.2% share ten years before. The presence of Hispanics among workers rose in a similar manner (from 10.7 to 14.6%) during this time (these shares are not shown because they overlap so closely with their share among all adults). This information indicates that the economic conditions Hispanics face, including those in the labor market, have become an increasingly important component of the U.S. economy.

## LABOR MARKET EARNINGS

In light of their growing representation in the working-age population, an important issue to consider is how Hispanics fared during the decade with

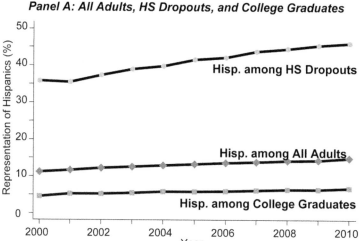

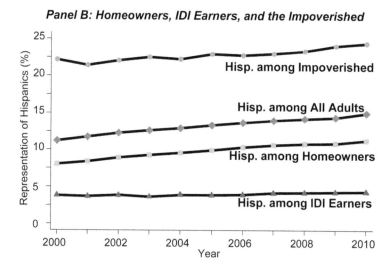

**Figure 1.1** Representation of Hispanics among Adults Ages 25-64 and among Specific Populations along Socioeconomic Dimensions: 2000-2010. *Source:* Authors' estimates using data from the 2000 PUMS and the 2001-2010 ACS in the IPUMS; only individuals ages 25–64 who resided outside of group quarters are included.

respect to income earned through wages, salaries, and self-employment income—a key labor market outcome. Throughout the past three decades, social scientists have consistently reported that Hispanics earn less on average than non-Hispanics, and our own estimates indicate this was still the case in 2010. As seen in Panel A in Table 1.1, Hispanics who were attached to the labor market (defined here as those who worked at least 20 hr per week for 27 or more weeks in the previous 12 months) earned an average of $34,900 ($16.90 per hour) in 2010, compared to $53,300 ($24.60 per hour) for non-Hispanics that year. Compared to their earnings in 2000, Hispanics lost ground during the decade when accounting for inflation using the Consumer Price Index, as their $28,600 income ($13.75 per hour) in 2000 was equivalent to over $36,000 ($17.40) in 2010. They also lost some ground relative to non-Hispanic workers, whose average labor market income levels rose near the inflation rate; the $41,800 ($19.14 per hour) earned by non-Hispanic Whites in 2000 was equivalent to $53,000 ($24.24) in 2010.

**TABLE 1.1  Economic, Demographic, and Socioeconomic Characteristics of Hispanic and Non-Hispanic Workers in 2000 and 2010**

| | Hispanics | | Non-Hispanics | |
|---|---|---|---|---|
| Characteristic | 2000 | 2010 | 2000 | 2010 |
| Panel A: Labor market income | | | | |
| Annual earned income | $28,570 | $34,901 | $41,822 | $53,336 |
| Hourly wages | $13.75 | $16.90 | $19.14 | $24.60 |
| *Ln*(hourly wages) | $2.39 | $2.60 | $2.67 | $2.93 |
| Panel B: Socioeconomic and demographic characteristics | | | | |
| Education (in years) | 10.49 | 11.22 | 13.47 | 13.77 |
| Less than high school | 45.1% | 35.4% | 11.8% | 8.0% |
| College graduate | 11.0% | 13.8% | 28.9% | 33.3% |
| Foreign-born | 58.5% | 58.2% | 9.6% | 11.6% |
| Years in U.S. if foreign-born | 16.13 | 18.7 | 18.23 | 20.14 |
| Limited English fluency | 29.5% | 29.3% | 1.6% | 1.7% |
| Potential experience (in years) | 23.78 | 24.53 | 24.57 | 26.03 |
| Panel C: Other economic outcomes | | | | |
| Owns a home | 51.0% | 51.6% | 73.4% | 71.5% |
| Has interest or dividend income | 7.17% | 3.3% | 22.8% | 12.8% |
| Average interest or dividend income, for those reporting it | $5,915 | $9,106 | $7,022 | $9,799 |
| Has health insurance | — | 58.6% | — | 84.1% |
| Below the poverty line | 18.1% | 19.6% | 8.0% | 10.7% |

*Source:* Author's estimates using the 2000 PUMS and the 2010 ACS in the IPUMS.

*Note:* The samples used here include individuals ages 25–64 who resided outside of group quarters. The sample sizes are 152,827 Hispanics in 2000; 196,026 Hispanics in 2010; 1,281,987 non-Hispanics in 2000; and 1,390,400 non-Hispanics in 2010. These samples represent 16.2 million, 24.1 million, 128.4 million, and 136.9 million adults, respectively. In Panel A, only individuals who worked at least 20 hr per week for 27 or more weeks in the previous 12 months are included.

Another way to identify their relative loss in earnings against non-Hispanics is through the change in the Hispanic/non-Hispanic wage differential (measured by the difference of the natural logarithm of hourly earnings between the two groups) during this time. On average, Hispanics earned 32.7% less than non-Hispanics in 2010, a wider differential than the 28.5% differential that existed a decade earlier. As we will discuss later in this chapter, however, basically all of the Hispanic/non-Hispanic wage differential can be explained by differences in education and other observable characteristics between the two populations.

## EDUCATION AND OTHER FORMS OF HUMAN CAPITAL

For decades, one of the primary explanations for the Hispanic/non-Hispanic earnings differential has been the relatively low levels of human capital among Hispanics. For example, based on data from the mid-1970s, economists Walter McManus, William Gould, and Finis Welch noted in their 1983 study that nearly all of the earnings disparities between Hispanic and non-Hispanic White men could be explained by differences in education, labor market experience, and English-language fluency. Decades later, such differences remained. To illustrate this point with regards to education, consider the over-representation of Hispanics among adults aged 25–64 without a high school diploma or equivalent, shown in the top panel of Figure 1.1. Hispanics represented 35.9% of this population in 2000, rising to 46.0% in 2010. This was a larger increase in magnitude during the decade than their increase among adults in general (10.1 vs. 3.7 percentage points), but a slightly smaller increase in relative terms (1.28 vs. 1.33 times). This indicates that the growing presence of Hispanics among adults who had not completed high school was driven by sheer population growth and not by an increase in the proportion of high school dropouts *within* the Hispanic population.

Figure 1.1 further shows that among college graduates in the same age range, the representation of Hispanics rose by a considerably low magnitude of 2.2 percentage points during the decade, from 4.6 to 6.8%. Still, in relative terms, the presence of Hispanics among college graduates was nearly 1.5 times greater in 2010 than in 2000, suggesting that among Hispanic adults, the share of college graduates increased.

Indeed, these patterns are supported in Panel B of Table 1.1. Hispanic adults had lower average education levels than non-Hispanics (11.2 years vs. 13.8 years in 2010), but this gap narrowed in the first decade of the millennium; the increase in average schooling by 0.7 years among Hispanics during this time exceeded the 0.3 year increase among non-Hispanics. Also, 45% of Hispanics had less than a high school education in 2000, but ten years later; this share had dropped by nearly ten percentage points. Only 11% of Hispanics had at least a four-year college degree in 2000, a proportion which increased to 13.8% at the end of the decade.

While these shares point to the under-education of Hispanics vis-à-vis non-Hispanics (a third of whom were college graduates in 2010), they indicate that Hispanics made some progress in narrowing the schooling attainment gap during the decade. Without this progress, the Hispanic/non-Hispanic earnings differential would likely have been wider in 2010. "Back-of-the-envelope" estimates support this inference. If Hispanics had the same shares of high school dropouts and college graduates in 2010 as they had in 2000, our estimates reveal they should have earned an average of $33,400 ($15.03 per hour) in 2010—$1,500 ($1.87 per hour) less than the labor market income they accrued that year.[2]

This is not to say that educational attainment no longer represents a challenge for Hispanic populations. As long as they have below-average schooling levels, the earnings and other economic outcomes of Hispanic Americans will likely remain below those of non-Hispanics. In fact, later in this chapter, we show that education plays a major role in explaining Hispanic/non-Hispanic differentials in wages and other economic status measures.

A lot of the education disparities between Hispanics and non-Hispanics relate to the large share of immigrants among Hispanic adults. As Table 1.1 shows, immigrants represented 58.2% of Hispanics in 2010, compared to 11.6% among non-Hispanics. Hispanic immigrants had an average of 10.1 years of schooling that year, and nearly half (48.3%) did not have a high school diploma. These relatively low education levels reduce the average schooling levels of Hispanics in general. It should be noted, however, that even if the schooling levels were similar between immigrants and natives, the larger share of immigrants among Hispanics versus non-Hispanics suggests that the earnings of Hispanics might still lag behind that of other populations. Social scientists, including Stephen Trejo (2003) and Barry Chiswick (1978), have found that education obtained abroad tends to be valued less in U.S. labor markets than schooling acquired in the United States.

Moreover, immigrants are not the only reason behind the relative under-education of Hispanics, as U.S.-born Hispanics also have less education on average than other Americans (12.7 vs. 13.7 years in 2010), and 17.4 versus 7.5% were high school dropouts. As Mark Hugo López discusses in the following chapter, the relatively low schooling investments made by Hispanics seem to be driven more by issues related to the need to support one's family instead of beliefs that education lacks value. Because better paying jobs tend to be filled by workers with a college education (or higher)—a trend unlikely to be reversed—Hispanic U.S. natives will likely fall further behind other U.S.-born workers with respect to their economic outcomes.[3] It follows that, in light of their population growth, policies designed to keep Hispanic youths in school will likely have larger long-term implications for national economic conditions than in the past.

Besides education, immigration relates to other human capital issues as well, including U.S. tenure and the ability to communicate in the English language. As seen in Table 1.1, Hispanic immigrants had resided in the country for less time than their non-Hispanic counterparts (about 18.7 years for foreign-born Hispanics compared to 20.1 years for foreign-born non-Hispanics in 2010). Immigration also explains the relatively low rates of English-language fluency among Hispanics, defined here as being able to speak the English language at least "well." Nearly 30% of Hispanic adults were not fluent in the English language, compared to less than 2% of non-Hispanics. Both of these components tend to compound the effects of lower education on Hispanic/non-Hispanic earnings differentials. For example, a host of studies reports how immigrants' earnings tend to increase the longer they reside in the United States, and they are enhanced by the ability to communicate in the English language.[4]

## OTHER ECONOMIC STATUS MEASURES

The bottom panel of Figure 1.1 presents the share of Hispanics among several sub-populations associated with various socioeconomic status indicators: homeowners, adults with interest or dividend income, and the impoverished (defined as those with family income falling below the federal poverty threshold).[5] This figure indicates that Hispanics were under-represented among higher socioeconomic-status groups and over-represented among the impoverished throughout the decade. However, these data also suggest that Hispanics seemingly gained some ground with respect to their *relative* economic status during the first decade of the millennium when considering homeownership tendencies and their presence among adults living in poverty.

### Homeownership

To illustrate, the share of Hispanics among homeowners rose 1.4 times during the decade (to 11.3% in 2010), which was a slightly higher growth, proportionately, than their increase among adults in general. This indicates that the rising representation of Hispanics among homeowners was driven by both population growth as well as a relative improvement in their homeownership rates vis-à-vis non-Hispanics. Indeed, our estimates in Table 1.1

(Panel C) show that these rates marginally rose (from 51.0 to 51.6%) for Hispanics between 2000 and 2010, while they fell slightly during the decade (from 73.4 to 71.5%) for non-Hispanics.

## Interest and Dividend Income Earners

Focusing on individuals who reported positive levels of interest or dividend income (IDI) in Figure 1.1, Hispanics lost some ground during the decade, as their presence in this group only rose by half a percentage point (about 1.1 times) in the decade, to 4.3% in 2010. Because this rise is less than their increase in representation among adults in general, Hispanic population growth—and not an increase in the share of IDI earners among Hispanics—appears to be responsible for their slightly larger presence among IDI earners by the end of the decade.

This conclusion is further supported by changes in the share of those accruing positive interest or dividend income among Hispanics versus non-Hispanics between 2000 and 2010 observed in Panel C in Table 1.1. The representation of IDI earners for both Hispanics and non-Hispanics fell sharply in the decade, from 7.2 to 3.3% for the former, and 22.8 to 12.8% among the latter. Note that Hispanics experienced the larger proportionate decline, as their share of IDI earners (which was small to begin with) fell by more than half compared to a 44% decline among non-Hispanics. However, among adults reporting this type of income, Hispanics narrowed the IDI gap with non-Hispanics between 2000 and 2010. This information suggests some progress made by Hispanics within this relative high socio-economic status population, as the average IDI rose by a larger margin for Hispanic IDI earners (from $5,915 to $9,106) than for non-Hispanics ($7,022 to $9,799). The importance of studying IDI in the context of an economic status indicator is due to the fact that it reflects asset and wealth accumulation that might not be picked up by labor market earnings or homeownership.

## Impoverishment

Figure 1.1 further shows that the share of Hispanics among adults living below the poverty line grew by about 1.1 times (from 22.2 to 24.4%) between 2000 and 2010. This under-proportionate growth (versus their share among all adults) indicates that Hispanic population growth, and not deterioration in their poverty position *relative* to non-Hispanics, explains their expanding presence among the impoverished in the decade. The poverty rates shown in Table 1.1 (Panel C) are consistent with this inference. While

Hispanics have considerably higher poverty rates than non-Hispanics (19.6 vs. 10.7% in 2010), the 1.5 percentage-point rise in the Hispanic poverty rate between 2000 and 2010 fell short, both in absolute and relative terms, of the 2.7 percentage-point rise in the non-Hispanic poverty rate. Given the importance of poverty rates in policy arenas, more detailed analyses of socioeconomic and demographic factors related to Hispanic poverty will be addressed by Mary Lopez in Chapter 4, and Carlos Siordia and Ruben Farias in Chapter 5. It should be noted here that the relatively high poverty rates among Hispanics partly stem from their below-average education levels and high shares of immigrants.

## Health Insurance Coverage

An additional socioeconomic status indicator pertains to health insurance coverage. Such information has been more difficult to analyze at the national level for specific demographic populations than other traditional measures (like earnings and homeownership) due to the lack of publicly available detailed datasets. Starting in 2008, however, health insurance coverage has been reported in the American Community Survey. While we cannot identify the time-trend for Hispanics with respect to this economic indicator for the decade, in the years this information has been reported, Hispanics have lagged behind their non-Hispanic counterparts. As reported in the last row of Table 1.1, only 58.6% of Hispanic adults between the ages of 25 and 64 had some type of health insurance in 2010, compared to 84.1% of their non-Hispanic counterparts. Explanations for the health insurance under-coverage of Hispanics will be discussed later in this volume by Jillian Medeiros and Gabriel Sanchez in Chapter 7. As they point out, education, immigration, and the types of jobs in which Hispanics work represent key factors.

## THE RELATIVE ECONOMIC STATUS OF HISPANICS BEFORE AND AFTER THE GREAT RECESSION

Some of the discussion thus far indicates that Hispanics made progress with respect to narrowing the gap with non-Hispanics for certain economic outcomes between 2000 and 2010. However, comparing these two years alone might obscure changes in the relative status of Hispanics during the Great Recession. As noted in the Preface, this recession technically started in December 2007 and ended in June 2009. It is not surprising that many of the economic status measures considered here deteriorated for both Hispanics and non-Hispanics between 2007 and 2010.

**TABLE 1.2 Explanations for the Hispanic/Non-Hispanic Differentials in Earnings and Other Economic Outcomes in 2010 (Reported as Percentage Points**

| Economic Outcome | Total Gap (Hispanic–Non-Hispanic) | Gap Explained by Education | Gap Explained by Other Observable Traits | Unexplained Gap |
|---|---|---|---|---|
| Panel A: Outcomes for all Hispanics | | | | |
| *ln*(hourly wages) | −32.68 | −28.01 | −4.56 | −0.12 |
| Homeownership | −19.88 | −5.39 | −11.17 | −3.32 |
| Interest, dividend income | −9.56 | −4.67 | −2.12 | −2.77 |
| Health insurance | −25.42 | −8.02 | −7.98 | −9.42 |
| Panel B: Ln(wages) by Hispanic subgroup | | | | |
| Mexican American | −37.38 | −33.77 | −4.58 | 0.97 |
| Puerto Rican | −13.70 | −10.75 | 1.17 | −4.11 |
| Cuban | −17.49 | −6.25 | −2.92 | −8.32 |
| Salvadoran | −45.02 | −47.56 | −9.13 | 11.67 |
| Panel C: Homeownership by Hispanic subgroup | | | | |
| Mexican American | −18.04 | −6.51 | −11.38 | −0.15 |
| Puerto Rican | −25.22 | −2.56 | −4.80 | −17.87 |
| Cuban | −10.63 | −1.36 | −5.32 | −3.95 |
| Salvadoran | −35.94 | −13.67 | −12.98 | −9.29 |
| Panel D: IDI earners by Hispanic subgroup | | | | |
| Mexican American | −10.19 | −5.65 | −2.08 | −2.45 |
| Puerto Rican | −8.72 | −2.98 | −1.18 | −4.57 |
| Cuban | −7.77 | −1.31 | −1.73 | −4.72 |
| Salvadoran | −10.54 | −6.88 | −2.47 | −1.20 |
| Panel E: Health insurance coverage by Hispanic subgroup | | | | |
| Mexican American | −29.46 | −9.68 | −8.29 | −11.49 |
| Puerto Rican | −3.89 | −3.49 | −0.24 | −0.16 |
| Cuban | −19.85 | −1.96 | −9.97 | −7.91 |
| Salvadoran | −35.94 | −13.67 | −12.98 | −9.29 |

*Source:* Authors' estimates using the 2010 ACS in the IPUMS.

*Notes:* The samples include individuals ages 25–64 who resided outside of group quarters. See Note 6 for more on the "explained" versus "unexplained" gaps with non-Hispanics, as well as for the list of "other observ. traits". For the earnings analyses, only individuals who worked at least 20 hr per week for 27 or more weeks in the previous 12 months are included. Due to rounding, the sum of the last three columns might not equal the first column.

In some cases, these declines were more pronounced for Hispanics. For example, homeownership rates fell by 2.7 percentage points (from 54.3% in 2007) among Hispanics, compared to a 2.3 percentage-point decline (from 73.8%) among non-Hispanics. Also, the share of IDI earners fell by 0.8 percentage points (from 4.1%) among Hispanics between 2007 and 2010; this was a larger decrease in proportionate terms than the 3.1 percentage-point fall in this share (from 15.5%) among non-Hispanics. These figures suggest that the Great Recession hit the wealth and asset accumulation potential of Hispanics particularly hard. This suggestion fits with a 2011 Pew Social & Demographic Trends report by Rakesh Kochhar, Richard Fry, and Paul Taylor showing that the median wealth of Hispanics fell by a larger percentage than that of other major racial/ethnic groups during the Great Recession.

For other outcomes, however, Hispanics did not lose ground against non-Hispanics. To illustrate, adult poverty rates for both groups rose in a proportionate manner between 2007 and 2010, from 16.1 to 19.6% among Hispanics, and from 8.7 to 10.7% among non-Hispanics. As such, the ratio of Hispanic/non-Hispanic adult poverty rates was about the same in 2010 (1.83) as in 2007 (1.85). Moreover, average hourly wages increased by 4% for Hispanics, but 3% for non-Hispanics, slightly narrowing the Hispanic/non-Hispanic earnings differential during this time. It therefore appears that the Great Recession did not have an "across-the-board" effect on the relative economic status of Hispanics.

## EFFECTS OF EDUCATION AND OTHER CHARACTERISTICS ON HISPANIC ECONOMIC OUTCOMES

The fact that various economic outcomes among Hispanics fall below those of non-Hispanics is consistent with their relatively low human capital levels. What remains unclear is how much differences in education and other characteristics contribute to Hispanic/non-Hispanic differentials in economic status indicators. More meaningful measures of the relative economic status of Hispanics should therefore consider "explained" versus "unexplained" (or skill-adjusted) differentials between Hispanics and non-Hispanics.

Panel A in Table 1.2 presents our estimates of these components for 2010 with respect to four economic outcomes: labor market earnings among workers attached to the labor market, homeownership rates, the share of adults with positive interest or dividend income, and health insurance coverage rates. We do not analyze poverty rates in this manner here because they are examined in considerable detail by Mary Lopez (in Chapter 4) and Carlos Siodia and Ruben Farias (in Chapter 5).

The first column shows the total differential in the economic status measures between Hispanics and non-Hispanics. The second column reveals the amount of the differential explained by differences in education between the two groups, while the third column presents how much of the Hispanic/non-Hispanic gap can be explained through differences in other observable characteristics. These "other" characteristics include socioeconomic and demographic traits often considered important determinants of economic outcomes, including gender, limited-English fluency, U.S.- versus foreign-born, immigrants' U.S. tenure, and potential labor market experience.[6] The final column contains the estimated Hispanic/non-Hispanic differential that was not accounted for by observable traits (i.e., the "unexplained" gap).

## Effects on Wages

The first row in Table 1.2 shows that on average, Hispanics earned 32.7% less per hour than non-Hispanics in 2010. Of this wage gap, differences in education between the two groups accounted for the vast majority (28.0 percentage points), indicating the importance of this human capital variable in generating labor market income. Other observable characteristics explained an additional 4.6 percentage points, leaving a trivial (and not statistically significant) unexplained wage gap of 0.1 percentage points. This information indicates that basically all of the Hispanic/non-Hispanic earnings differential in 2010 was driven by human capital, socioeconomic, and demographic features.

We realize that many studies in labor economics separate men from women while analyzing earnings because of underlying differences in labor force participation rates between the two groups. Previous scholars, including Irene Browne (1999) have also reported smaller racial/ethnic earnings disparities among women than men. Moreover, as we have found elsewhere (e.g., Mora & Dávila, 2006, 1998), the returns to skill, including English-language proficiency, differ between Hispanic men and women. While we include gender as one of the observable traits, perhaps our results mask distinct gender-related differences in the explained versus unexplained components of the Hispanic/non-Hispanic wage differential.

A closer examination of the data (not reported in the table to conserve space) indicates that Hispanic women had a smaller earnings differential vis-à-vis non-Hispanic women (28.0%) than their male counterparts (38.2%) in 2010. As with Hispanics in general, differences in education explained the vast part of the earnings disparity for both groups, contributing 22.5 percentage points to the Hispanic/non-Hispanic wage differential for women that year, and 32.4 percentage points for men. Observable characteristics accounted for another 3.9 percentage points of this earnings differential for women and 6.9 points for men.

This means that Hispanic women earned an estimated 1.6% less than otherwise similar non-Hispanic women in 2010, while Hispanic men earned 1.1% more than their non-Hispanic male counterparts. Exactly why Hispanic women had a slight wage penalty while Hispanic men had a slight wage premium versus their non-Hispanic peers is not something we can easily explain.[7] However, for both groups, these unexplained earnings differences are relatively small, such that they might not warrant as much policy attention as Hispanic/non-Hispanic disparities in other socioeconomic outcomes, such as educational attainment.

## Effects on Other Economic Status Measures

The Hispanic homeownership rate of 51.6% was 19.9 percentage points below the rate for non-Hispanics in 2010. While sizeable, five-sixths of this homeownership gap can be explained by differences in observable characteristics between Hispanics and non-Hispanics, as seen in Table 1.2. Education accounted for over a quarter (5.4 points) of this gap, and other characteristics accounted for over half (11.2 points). Controlling for these characteristics therefore reveals that the unexplained homeownership rates between Hispanics and non-Hispanics only varied by 3.3 percentage points.

Similarly, human capital, demographic, and socioeconomic characteristics explained much of the Hispanic/non-Hispanic differential in the share of income and dividend earners in 2010. The share of IDI earners among Hispanics was 9.6 percentage points less than their share among non-Hispanics that year, but after accounting for schooling differences (which explained 4.7 percentage points of this differential) and other characteristics (which accounted for an additional 2.1 points), this gap shrinks to 2.8 percentage points.

Sixteen percentage points (slightly under two-thirds) of the 25.4 percentage-point under-coverage of health insurance among Hispanics versus non-Hispanics in 2010 can be equally explained by differences in education and other features. Other studies have pointed to education and immigration as key reasons for the lack of health insurance among Hispanics. While our results suggest that these characteristics account for a significant part of the difference, a substantial unexplained gap—about 9.4 percentage points—remained between Hispanics and non-Hispanics. Later in this volume, issues related to Hispanic health outcomes will be discussed by Jillian

Medeiros and Gabriel Sanchez in Chapter 7 as well as by Veronica Salinas and her co-authors in Chapter 8.

## HISPANIC SUB-ETHNIC HETEROGENEITY AND ECONOMIC OUTCOMES

Our discussion thus far indicates that Hispanics as a group differ from non-Hispanics on a variety of socioeconomic and demographic dimensions, including differences in the representation of immigrants. It should also be noted that *within* the Hispanic population considerable heterogeneity exists, extending far beyond basic differences typically associated with immigrants versus U.S. natives. To illustrate, in a 2010 Census Brief, Sharon Ennis, Merarys Ríos-Vargas, and Nora Albert estimated that Mexican Americans (including Mexican immigrants) represented nearly two-thirds (63%) of all Hispanics living in the 50 states or DC, followed by Puerto Ricans (9.2%), Cubans (3.5%), Salvadorans (3.3%), Dominicans (2.8%), and Guatemalans (2.1%), with other smaller Hispanic sub-groups comprising the remaining 16.1%. Often, the use of the term "Hispanic" thus masks important differences along demographic, socioeconomic, and cultural dimensions across various Hispanic subgroups.

Given this heterogeneity, "one-size-fits-all" policies designed with "Hispanics" in mind will likely have different effects across the specific Hispanic groups. To illustrate, consider issues related to immigration. Island-born Puerto Ricans are U.S. citizens at birth. As such, the only Puerto Rican immigrants are those born outside of the United States and its territories who identify themselves as Puerto Rican; these individuals represented only 2.5% of Puerto Rican adults of traditional working ages in the U.S. mainland in 2010. That same year, immigrants represented almost six out of ten Mexican Americans (58.4%) between the ages of 25 and 64 (about the share as for Hispanics in general), seven out of ten Cubans (70.6%), and more than nine out of ten Salvadorans (92.1%). It follows that Puerto Ricans likely have different perspectives on immigration than other Hispanic populations. Even comparing immigrants across these groups raises issues, given that Mexican immigrants tend to migrate to the United States for economic purposes, while Cuban immigrants (and in certain recent time periods, Salvadorans) have migrated as political refugees.

Moreover, with differences in the composition of immigrants (and reasons for migration) come differences in schooling attainment, which in turn have implications for the economic outcomes of specific Hispanic populations. Of the four largest subgroups, Cubans have the highest average level of education (13.1 years in 2010), followed by Puerto Ricans (12.5 years), Mexican Americans (10.7 years), and Salvadorans (9.6 years).

Regional heterogeneity also exists. Mexican Americans have tradition-
ally settled in the Southwestern United States, although this population
has been dispersing into non-traditional areas, such as the South, in recent years. Puerto Ricans and Dominicans tend to live in the Northeastern
United States, while Cubans are concentrated in Florida; in fact, over two-
thirds of all Cuban American adults aged 25–64 reside in the state. Local
and regional economic conditions can therefore have different impacts on
specific Hispanic groups.

   This heterogeneity along a variety of dimensions highlights the difficulty
in assessing the economic status of Hispanic subgroups based on the status
of Hispanics overall, as the pan-ethnic experiences might not be the same
for specific segments of the Hispanic American population. We therefore
examine the main economic indicators discussed in this chapter separately
for the four largest Hispanic subgroups: Mexican Americans, Puerto Ricans, Cubans, and Salvadorans. These findings are presented in Panels B–E
in Table 1.2.

## Wages of the Four Largest Hispanic Groups

   In terms of Hispanic/non-Hispanic earnings differentials, Panel B in
Table 1.2 indicates considerable differences across the four populations in
2010. Salvadorans had the largest "raw" wage disparity with non-Hispanics
(45%), and Puerto Ricans had the smallest one (13.7%). Consistent with
the rank order of average educational attainment, schooling differences
explained the largest portion of the Hispanic/non-Hispanic earnings differential for the least educated group (Salvadorans), followed by Mexican
Americans (the group with the second lowest schooling levels), then Puerto
Ricans, and Cubans.

   Moreover, the positive "unexplained" wage gap among Salvadorans reported in this table suggests that, given their education levels and other
characteristics, they earned 11.7% *more* than comparable non-Hispanics,
faring better than the other three Hispanic subgroups in 2010, other things
the same. Furthermore, the considerable wage penalty of 37.4% accrued
by Mexican Americans versus non-Hispanics virtually disappears when accounting for differences in observable characteristics. Cubans, and to a
lesser extent, Puerto Ricans, continued to earn less (8.3 and 4.1% less, respectively) than comparable non-Hispanic workers.

   It therefore appears that the relatively low average earnings observed for
Mexican Americans and Salvadorans in 2010 were primarily driven by their
relatively low levels of human capital and other observable characteristics,
and not by unmeasured circumstances in the labor market (such as limited
geographic and occupational mobility, monopsonistic power of their em-

ployers, or labor market discrimination). Given that the wages of Cubans and Puerto Ricans remained below those of the non-Hispanic counterparts after controlling for other traits, we cannot draw the same conclusion for these two Hispanic subgroups at this time. These findings suggest that an increase in the average schooling level of Hispanics (perhaps facilitated through adult education programs, given their high share of immigrants) might have a particularly acute impact on the relative earnings of Mexican Americans and Salvadorans.

## Homeownership Rates of the Four Largest Hispanic Groups

Homeownership rates among adults ages 25–64 also varied across the four Hispanic subgroups in 2010, with Cubans having the highest rate (60.9% = 10.6 percentage points below the 71.5% homeownership rate of non-Hispanics), followed by Mexican Americans (53.5% = 18.0 percentage points below non-Hispanics), and Salvadorans and Puerto Ricans (as home-owners represented less than 47% in both groups). As seen in Panel C in Table 1.2, for all of the sub-ethnic populations except Puerto Ricans, education and other features explained a considerable portion of the homeown-ership disparities compared to non-Hispanics.

This was especially the case for the two groups with the lowest schooling levels: Salvadorans (as education contributed 8.9 percentage points to their homeownership differential with non-Hispanics) and Mexican Americans (with education accounting for 6.5 percentage points). In fact, for these two groups, when further considering other observable attributes, their homeownership gaps with non-Hispanics evaporate. That is, the relative-ly low homeownership rates among Salvadorans and Mexican Americans appears to stem from their human capital and other socioeconomic and demographic characteristics, and not from unmeasured factors. This was not the case for Puerto Ricans, as these characteristics explained less than one-third of their homeownership rate differential with non-Hispanics. This Hispanic subgroup might therefore be particularly sensitive to policies related to homeownership.

These results indicate that improvements in the educational attainment of Hispanics would likely yield heterogeneous outcomes on homeownership tendencies across Hispanic sub-ethnic groups. For Salvadorans and Mexican Americans, additional education could go a long way in terms of narrowing their homeownership gap with non-Hispanics, but it might have less of an ef-fect on this economic status measure for Puerto Ricans and Cubans.

## Interest Income Earners among Four Largest Hispanic Groups

The shares of the four largest Hispanic subgroups in 2010 who reported interest and dividend income were closer together than the other economic indicators considered in Table 1.2. These shares ranged from 2.3% among Salvadorans (10.5 percentage points below the 12.8% share of non-Hispanic IDI earners) to 5.1% among Cubans (7.8 percentage points below the non-Hispanic IDI share).

Nevertheless, as with the other economic status measures, the relationship between the likelihood of having IDI income and education (and other characteristics) varied considerably across these populations. Panel D in Table 1.2 shows that education and other observable features explained almost nine-tenths of the Hispanic/non-Hispanic gap in the share of IDI earners for Salvadorans (9.4 out of 10.5 percentage points), and three-quarters of this gap for Mexican Americans (7.7 out of 10.2 percentage points). In contrast, such characteristics accounted for less than half of this IDI differential for Puerto Ricans (4.2 out of 8.7 percentage points) and about 40% for Cubans (3.1 out of 7.8 percentage points) in 2010.

Similar to the earnings and homeownership discussion above, education appears to be a stronger explanatory component in the relatively low share of IDI earners for Salvadorans and Mexican Americans than for Puerto Ricans and Cubans, at least in 2010. As such, education policies designed for "Hispanics" in general could differently alter the relative economic standing across various Hispanic subgroups.

## Health Insurance among the Four Largest Hispanic Groups

The four largest Hispanic subgroups also have dissimilar rates of health insurance coverage, suggesting that policies related to mandated health insurance would have disparate impacts across Hispanic populations. Four out of five Puerto Rican adults had health insurance in 2010, a coverage rate only about 4 percentage points below the one for non-Hispanics. Recall that nearly all Puerto Rican adults on the U.S. mainland are U.S. citizens, and they seem to display similar propensities as other U.S. natives with respect to the likelihood of acquiring health insurance. In fact, as Panel E in Table 1.2 shows, when controlling for education and other characteristics, the gap between Puerto Ricans and non-Hispanics essentially disappears.

Cubans had the next highest health insurance coverage rate (64.2%, which was 19.9 percentage points below the non-Hispanic rate), followed by Mexican Americans (54.6%), and Salvadorans (48.1%). Note that this ranking mirrors the differences in average education levels mentioned above. Accounting for human capital and other characteristics explains about three-quarters of the Hispanic/non-Hispanic gaps in health insurance coverage rates for Salvadorans (as education and other traits accounted for 26.7 of the 35.9 percentage-point gap with non-Hispanics), and 60% for both Mexican Americans (18.0 of 29.5 percentage points) and Cubans (11.9 of 19.9 percentage points).

Nevertheless, because the total Hispanic/non-Hispanic differentials in health insurance coverage are large in magnitude for these three groups, the unexplained differences are also sizeable. For example, in 2010, a double-digit difference (11.5 percentage points) existed in health insurance coverage rates between Mexican Americans and otherwise similar non-Hispanics, a difference unexplained by education levels, immigration, and other attributes. As such, health-related policies might be of particular interest to this Hispanic group.

## CONCLUSION

In the first decade of the new millennium, the rapid growth of the Hispanic population in the United States raised the significance of understanding and monitoring this group's economic status. We have analyzed several of their economic outcomes in this chapter, including labor market earnings, homeownership rates, the likelihood of having interest and dividend income, and health insurance coverage. With respect to each of these measures, Hispanics as a group tend to lag behind non-Hispanics on average. The relatively low educational attainment of Hispanics represents one of the key explanations behind these disparities. On a more encouraging note, we also show that Hispanics made progress in terms of narrowing their education gap with non-Hispanics between 2000 and 2010. If this tendency continues, given the sheer size of the Hispanic population, such schooling improvements should not only enhance the average economic status of Hispanics—they should enhance the economic output of the nation overall. With that said, under-education among Hispanics remains a challenge (even for U.S.-born Hispanics), and one that appears worthy of policy attention.

We also discuss how the Hispanic population is far from being homogeneous, a fact often overlooked when researchers and policymakers consider "Hispanics." This heterogeneity exists along demographic lines [such as with the various sub-ethnic groups (some of whom have roots going back before the United States existed), culture, immigration, reasons for migration, geographic settlement patterns, and so forth] as well as along socioeconomic dimensions. (Such heterogeneity will be further discussed in subsequent chapters.) Policies, including those related to education, designed to improve the economic outcomes of "Hispanics" as a standardized group might therefore have dissimilar effects across various segments of the Hispanic population. It follows that such policies might be more effective if they are specifically framed to account for the heterogeneity of Hispanic Americans.

## NOTES

1. Unless otherwise noted, our estimates in this chapter are based on adults ages 25–64 who resided outside of group quarters in the 2000 Public Use Micro data Sample (PUMS) and the 2001–2010 American Community Surveys (ACS), made available in the Integrated Public Use Micro data Series (IPUMS) by Ruggles et al., (2012). See the Data Appendix chapter for more information on these datasets.

2. We obtained these estimates by applying the 2000 education distribution of Hispanics attached to the labor market to their 2010 counterparts. Average wages can be partitioned into the weighted averages of wages earned by high school dropouts, college graduates, and other workers: Average Wage = a(Average Wage$_{HS\_Dropout}$) + b(Average Wage$_{College+}$) + c(Average Wage$_{Other}$) , where "a," "b," and "c" (which sum to one) represent the shares of Hispanic workers with less than a high school education, a college education or more, and high school graduates (including those who started but did not complete college). For Hispanic workers in 2000, the values of "a," "b," and "c" were 38.69%, 13.46%, and 47.85%, respectively. In 2010, the average earnings of Hispanic workers were $23,696 ($8.89 per hour) among high school dropouts; $60,518 ($27.80) among college graduates; and $33,712 ($16.41) among other workers.

3. As reported by Christopher Goodman and Steven Mance (2011), total nonfarm employment fell by 5.4% between December 2007 and June 2009—the Great Recession. Jobs were lost in all major industries during this time except for in education and health care services (which experienced an employment increase of 3.3%), the government, and utilities. Jobs in these industries often require relatively high levels of education, such that the employment opportunities for less educated populations tended to be hit particularly hard by the recession.

4. For examples, see Chiswick (1978); McManus, Gould, & Welch (1983); Chiswick & Miller (1995); Mora and Dávila (1998, 2006); and Trejo (2003).

5. The federal government establishes the poverty thresholds, which vary with respect to the size of the family. One caveat with using these thresholds is that they are not adjusted for regional cost-of-living differences. As such, some families in low-cost areas with income levels below the poverty threshold might be better off in terms of their standard of living than families in high-cost areas with income levels just above the threshold. We do not attempt to address this caveat here, nor do the other studies in this volume exploring poverty issues, but the reader should realize this caveat exists.

6. Specifically, these characteristics include limited-English proficiency, U.S.-versus foreign-born, the U.S. tenure of immigrants, potential experience, experience-squared, paid- versus self-employment, gender, race [White (base),

Black, Native American, Asian, and other/mixed], and geographic region [New England, North Central, South Central, Middle Atlantic, South Atlantic, Mountain, and Pacific (base)]. When analyzing earnings, we only consider individuals who were "attached" to the labor market—those who worked for at least 20 hr per week for 27 or more weeks. When analyzing the likelihood of being a homeowner, having positive interest or dividend income, and having health insurance, we further included in the "other" characteristics whether the person was employed, was married, and the number of the individual's children who resided in the household. To obtain the estimates explained by these characteristics, we utilized Oaxaca-type decomposition (e.g., Oaxaca, 1973) by first regressing the economic outcome on the set of observable characteristics for non-Hispanics only, using ordinary least squares for the natural logarithm of earnings, and probit regression for the other economic outcomes. We then applied these regression estimates to Hispanics to predict what their economic outcome should have been, given their characteristics. The difference between the predicted outcomes for Hispanics and non-Hispanics provided the Hispanic/non-Hispanic differential explained by differences in observable characteristics. The remainder of the differential represented the portion that was not explained by these characteristics. Details can be obtained from the authors.

7. We initially suspected that marital status and the presence of children were affecting these results, as these demographic features were not included in the set of "other" characteristics in our earnings analysis. However, we obtained a similar pattern when accounting for these traits (although the difference narrowed); as Hispanic women earned 1.1% less than their otherwise similar non-Hispanic counterparts and Hispanic men earned 1.0% more in 2010. We further considered that self-employment might be affecting the results, given that we have found elsewhere that the self-employment earnings and tendencies of Hispanic men and women changed differently during the 2000s (Dávila & Mora, 2012). We therefore excluded the self-employed from our analysis here and defined earnings solely based on wages and salaries. In this exercise, Hispanic men and women both earned less than their non-Hispanic peers in 2010, although Hispanic women continued to have a larger unexplained Hispanic/non-Hispanic earnings differential than men (4.2% vs. 1.9%).

## REFERENCES

Browne, I. (1999). Latinas and African American women in the U.S. labor market. In I. Browne (Ed.), *Latinas and African American women at work: Race, gender, and economic inequality* (pp. 1–31). New York: Russell Sage Foundation.

Chiswick, B. R. (1978). The effect of Americanization on the earnings of foreign-born men. *Journal of Political Economy, 86,* 897–921.

Chiswick, B. R., & Miller, P. W. (1995). The endogeneity between language and earnings: International analyses. *Journal of Labor Economics, 13*(2), 246–288.

Dávila, A., & Mora, M. T. (in press). *Hispanic entrepreneurs in the 2000s.* Palo Alto: Stanford University Press.

Ennis, S. R., Ríos-Vargas, M., & Albert, N. G. (2011, May). The U.S. Hispanic population: 2010. *2010 Census Briefs.* Washington: U.S. Census Bureau.

Goodman, C. J., & Mance, S. M. (2011, April). Employment loss and the 2007–09 recession. *Monthly Labor Review,* 3–12.

Kochhar, R., Fry, R., & Taylor P. (2011, July 26). *Wealth gaps rise to record highs between Whites, Blacks and Hispanics.* Washington, DC: Pew Social & Demographic Trends, www.pewsocialtrends.org.

McManus, W. S., Gould, W., & Welch, F. (1983). Earnings of Hispanic men: The role of English language proficiency. *Journal of Labor Economics, 1*(2), 101–130.

Mora, M. T., & Dávila, A. (2006). Hispanic ethnicity, gender, and the change in the LEP-earnings penalty in the U.S. during the 1990s. *Social Science Quarterly, 87*(5), 1295–1318.

Mora, M. T., & Dávila, A. (1998). Gender, earnings, and the English-skill acquisition of Hispanic workers in the United States. *Economic Inquiry, 36*(4), 631–644.

Oaxaca, R. (1973). Male-female wage differentials in urban labor markets, *International Economic Review, 14,* 693–709.

Passel, J., Cohn, D., & López, M. H. (2011). *Census 2010: 50 million Latinos Hispanics Account for more than half of nation's growth in past decade.* Washington, D.C.: Pew Hispanic Center, Available at: http://www.pewhispanic.org/files/reports/140.pdf .

Selig Center for Economic Growth. (2010). *The multicultural economy.* Athens, GA: University of Georgia, Terry College of Business.

Trejo, S. J. (2003). Intergenerational progress of Mexican-origin workers in the U.S. labor market. *Journal of Human Resources, 38*(3), 467–89.

CHAPTER 2

# EDUCATIONAL EXPECTATIONS AND REALITIES FOR YOUNG LATINOS

**Mark Hugo López**
*Pew Hispanic Center*

Economists and other social scientists have long established the economic benefits associated with greater educational attainment. Typically, each additional year of education is associated with earnings that are 8% higher or more—more education means more earnings. And, for those who hold a bachelor's degree or higher, education premiums are even greater (Goldin & Katz, 2007). A 2011 analysis by Paul Taylor and his colleagues in the Pew Social and Demographic Trends project at the Pew Research Center quantified the lifetime payoff to pursuing further education. According to that analysis, over the course of a 40-year work life, a high school graduate with no further education can expect to earn an inflation-adjusted $770,000. In contrast, pursuit of a postsecondary degree can substantially improve lifetime earnings. The average worker with an associate's degree, but no further education, earns about one million dollars over their 40-year work life. And the average worker with a bachelor's degree—but no advanced degree—earns about $1.4 million. However, going to college has costs—

*The Economic Status of the Hispanic Population*, pages 23–31
Copyright © 2013 by Information Age Publishing
All rights of reproduction in any form reserved.

both in tuition costs and foregone earnings. Taking these into account, the lifetime marginal payoff for a bachelor's degree over a high school diploma is $550,000.

Beyond earnings, more educational attainment is related to non-pecuniary benefits as well, including better health, work skill, social, and civic outcomes (e.g., Oreopoulos & Salvanes, 2011). Indeed, in a recent survey of college graduates, 74% said their college education was "very useful" in increasing their knowledge and helping them to grow intellectually. More than two-thirds (69%) said their college education was "very helpful" in helping them to grow and mature as a person (Taylor et al., 2011).

The benefits of a college education are not lost on America's youth—especially Latinos.[2] In a 2009 Pew Hispanic Center survey of Latinos, fully 89% of those aged 16 to 25 said a college degree was necessary for success in life, a share higher than among all American youths (82%). Among adults, Latinos are more likely than other adults to believe in the value of a college degree. Some 88% said a college degree is necessary for success in life while three-in-four (74%) of all U.S. adults said the same (López, 2009).

Latino parents too believe in the value of a college education. When asked what their parents said they should do after high school, 77% of young Latinos answered that going to college was the first thing their parents encouraged them to do (López, 2009). This was followed by "getting a job" (11%), and doing "whatever they wanted" (7%). In this respect, Latino parents are no different than other parents. When asked if their children would attend college, nearly all parents—whether non-Hispanic White, Black or Latino—said they expected their children to do so (Taylor et al., 2011).

None of these findings are new. For a few decades now, surveys have shown that parents have high educational expectations for their children. The same surveys have shown that young people, especially minority youth, see value in a college education (Schneider, Martinez, & Owens, 2006). More broadly, the issue of education is a top issue for Latinos. When asked to rate the personal importance of several issues such as immigration, the federal budget deficit, health care, the environment, and education, nearly six-in-ten (58%) Latino registered voters rated the issue of education as extremely important to them personally, ahead of all other issues (López, 2010). Education was followed by the issues of jobs (54%) and health care (51%). Among all Latino adults, nearly half (47%) said education was extremely important to them. No other issue rated this highly (López, Morin, & Taylor, 2010).

Over the decades, Latino educational attainment in the United States has been characterized by high dropout rates and low college completion rates (e.g., Kewal Ramani, Gilbertson, Fox, & Provasnik, 2007). However, both problems have moderated over time as more Latino youth are engaged in school, completing high school, going to college, and engaged in the workforce (Fry, 2009). Even so, an education gap remains between Latinos and non-Hispanic Whites.

At the same time, the Latino population has grown to become the nation's largest racial/ethnic minority group. It is also its youngest, with a median age of 27 compared with 41 for non-Hispanic Whites, 32 for Blacks, and 35 for Asians (Pew Hispanic Center, 2011). Overall, more than one-third of all Latinos are under the age 18. How these young people come of age will greatly impact the nation during this century.

## EDUCATIONAL EXPECTATIONS

Even though a college education is valued by Latino adults and youths, educational *expectations* among Latino youths are lower than might be expected. Based on an analysis of the 2009 National Survey of Latinos (described in this chapter's appendix) from the Pew Hispanic Center, when asked "How much farther in school do you plan to go?", just half (52%) of Latino 18-to-24 year-olds said they expect to get a college degree (see Table 2.1). In contrast, a similar survey of millennial youth from the Pew Research Center conducted in 2010 (also described in the chapter appendix) found that 73% of all youth ages 18 to 24 planned to get a bachelor's degree.

This finding, however, masks an immigration divide in educational expectations among Latino youths. Only one-third of immigrant Latinos ages 18–24 said they plan to get a college degree while six-in-ten (61%) of native-born young Latinos had the same plans. Young immigrant Latinos were also more likely to say they did not plan to continue their education. More than one-third (36%) said they did not have plans to go any further in school (López, 2009). In addition, while native-born Latinos have higher educational expectations than the foreign-born, compared to all youth, educational expectations among native-born Latino youths are lower.

**TABLE 2.1  Percent of Latino Youths and All Youths Ages 18 to 24 Expecting to Earn a Bachelors Degree or Higher**

| | | Latino Youth | | |
| Characteristic | All | Native Born | Foreign born | All Youth |
| --- | --- | --- | --- | --- |
| All youths | 52% | 61% | 34% | 73% |
| Currently enrolled in school | 79% | 82% | 69% | 82% |
| **Not in school, but plan to return** | **48%** | **49%** | **45%** | **60%** |

*Source:* Author's tabulations from the 2009 National Survey of Latinos, Pew Hispanic Center, and the 2010 Millennials Survey, Pew Research Center.

When considering the educational expectations of those currently enrolled in school, aims are high and Latino/non-Hispanic gaps are diminished (see Table 2.1). Among students ages 18–24, equal shares of Latinos (79%) and all young people (82%) said they plan to get a college degree. Of immigrant young Latinos enrolled in school, nearly seven-in-ten (69%) said they plan to attain this level of schooling. This share is lower than that among the native born (82%), but the immigrant/native gap in educational expectations is smaller among those currently enrolled in school than it is among all young Latinos.

In contrast to those in school, educational expectations are significantly lower among young people ages 18 to 24 that are not enrolled but plan to return to school. Fewer than half of Latinos (48%) in this group expected to get a college degree (see Table 2.1). Among all youths, 60% of the same group planned to get a college degree. However, while a gap in educational expectations exists among immigrant Latinos and native-born Latinos enrolled in school, of those who are not enrolled but plan to return, the gap is much smaller and statistically insignificant. In this group, 45% of immigrant young Latinos planned to get a college degree compared with 49% of native-born young Latinos.

Not all Latino young people intend to return to school. Among those ages 16 to 25 that were not in school, 41% said they did not intend to return. Of these, half were working full-time and an additional 17% were working part-time. For Latino youth outside of school not planning to return, 35% were married and two-thirds (66%) had children.

## SCHOOL ENROLLMENT

Despite the value Latinos place on a college education and the generally high, but lagging, educational expectations, a smaller share of young Latinos than non-Hispanics were enrolled in college. In 2009, just 29% of Latinos ages 18 to 24 were pursuing a college degree while 42% of all young people were enrolled in college (see Panel A in Table 2.2). Just as with educational expectations, an immigrant/native divide among young Latinos exists. Only 16% of immigrant Latinos were enrolled in college compared with 36% of native-born Latinos in 2009.

By contrast, the Latino/non-Hispanic gap in college enrollment rates was larger among the foreign-born—39 percentage points. In 2009, 55% of non-Hispanic immigrants ages 18 to 24 were enrolled in college. In 2000, the gap in college enrollment rates between young Latino and non-Hispanic immigrants was almost as wide. Then, 11% of foreign-born young Latinos were enrolled in college, compared to nearly half (48%) of their non-Hispanic counterparts—a 37 percentage point gap.

**TABLE 2.2   College Enrollment and Educational Attainment among Latino Youths, All Youths, and Foreign-Born Non-Hispanic Youths**

| Characteristic | Latinos | | | | Foreign-Born Non-Hispanics |
| | All | Native-Born | Foreign-Born | All Youth | |
| --- | --- | --- | --- | --- | --- |
| Panel A: College enrollment among 18 to 24 year olds in 2000 and 2009 | | | | | |
| Enrollment rate in 2009 | 29% | 36% | 16% | 42% | 55% |
| Enrollment rate in 2000 | 20% | 27% | 11% | 34% | 48% |
| Number enrolled in 2009 (in thousands) | 1,614 | 1,331 | 283 | 12,733 | 776 |
| Number enrolled in 2000 (in thousands) | 942 | 701 | 241 | 9,192 | 31 |
| Panel B: Educational attainment among 25 to 34 year olds in 2009 | | | | | |
| Less than 9th grade | 16% | 3% | 27% | 4% | 3% |
| 9th grade to 12th grade | 18% | 14% | 22% | 9% | 4% |
| High school graduate | 29% | 29% | 28% | 24% | 16% |
| GED | 4% | 5% | 2% | 4% | 2% |
| Some college | 19% | 36% | 15% | 32% | 24% |
| College graduate | 13% | 18% | 8% | 31% | 52% |

*Source:* Author's tabulations of the 2009 American Community Survey (1% IPUMS) and the 2000 Census (5% IPUMS).

*Notes:* "High school graduate" includes those who hold a GED. For Panel B, percentages may not sum to 100% due to rounding.

During the first decade of the 2000s, as the Latino population has grown, more young Latinos went to college. Some 1.6 million young Latinos were enrolled in college in 2009, up from 942,000 in 2000. But population growth alone does not explain recent gains in Latino college student enrollments. Between 2000 and 2009, the college enrollment rate among young Latinos increased nine percentage points, rising from 20 to 29%. This gain in enrollment rates was higher than for all young people. Between 2000 and 2009, the share of those ages 18 to 24 enrolled in college increased eight percentage points, from 34% in 2000 to 42% in 2009.

However, despite increases in enrollment rates and a greater number of college goers, the majority of young Latinos were not pursuing a college degree. When asked why they were not enrolled in school, the number one reason cited by young Latinos was the "need to support family." Some 74% of young non-student Latinos ages 16 to 25 gave this reason (López, 2009). This was followed by "English skills are limited" (49%), "don't like school" (42%), and "can't go on in school" (40%).

It is unclear, however, what the "need to support family" means. It could mean that a young Latino has a new family and is just getting started in life.

It could also mean that the young Latino needs to help his or her parents because one is ill, the family needs help making ends meet, or that the youth needs to support him/herself. Recent evidence suggests Latino youth are not alone in citing this reason. Among young people ages 18 to 34 without a college degree and who were not enrolled in school, two-thirds (67%) said the reason "need to support family" applies to them. This was followed by 57% who said they would rather work or make money (Taylor et al., 2011).

## EDUCATIONAL ATTAINMENT

Educational attainment among Latinos is lower than it is among all young people. Thirteen percent of Latinos ages 25 to 34 had a bachelor's degree in 2009, compared to 31% of all young adults (see Panel B in Table 2.2). By comparison, in 2000, 11% of Latinos ages 25 to 34 had a bachelor's degree, less than half of the 28% share of college graduates among all young people in this age range.

Once again, a divide along the lines of nativity is present among young Latinos. Some 18% of the native born had a college degree, while 8% of the foreign-born had one. Native-born Latinos were also more likely to have some college experience than foreign-born Latinos. More than half (54%) of native-born Latinos had attended or graduated from college, compared to just 23% of their foreign-born counterparts. Latino immigrants were also less likely to have completed high school, as nearly half (49%) did not have a high school diploma or equivalent versus 17% of the native-born.

By comparison, non-Hispanic immigrants had higher levels of educational attainment than Latino immigrants (see Panel B in Table 2.2). For example, more than half (52%) of non-Hispanic immigrants ages 25 to 34 had a bachelor's degree or more, a rate more than six times the 8% share among immigrant Latinos. Another 24% of non-Hispanic immigrants had completed some college, compared with 15% of Latino immigrants.

Even so, the number of young Latinos completing college has been increasing. In 2008–2009, a record 130,000 bachelor's degrees were awarded to Latinos in the 50 states and the District of Columbia, up from 19,000 in 1976–1977 (U.S. Department of Education, 2011). The share of all college degree recipients who are Latino has also increased, to 8% in 2008–2009, up from 2% in 1976–1977. Among Latinos who received college degrees in 2008–2009, six-in-ten (61%) were females.

The growth in the number of Latino college graduates partly reflects the greater number of college-age Latinos enrolled in school. However, even though the share of college degrees awarded to Latinos has reached a record high, it still lags their 18% share of the population ages 18–24 (according to tabulations from the 2009 ACS).

Latinos earn degrees in many of the same fields as non-Hispanics, according to an analysis of data from the 2009 American Community Survey. Among those ages 21 to 25—recent college graduates—20% of Latinos earned a degree in business fields, 11% in social science fields, 8% each in psychology and education, and 7% in engineering.

## LATINO HIGH SCHOOL DROPOUTS AND THE GED

While the number of Latinos in college is at an all-time high, as is the number awarded a bachelor's degree, among Latinos who do not have a high school diploma, few are continuing their education. One way for high school dropouts to pursue an education is with the General Education Development (GED) credential, an alternative to a high school diploma. High school dropouts who earn a GED are more likely to be employed and to earn more than high school dropouts who have not earned a GED (Fry, 2010).

Just one-in-ten (10%) of Latino high school dropouts had received a GED credential. By contrast, non-Hispanic White high school dropouts were three times more likely, and Blacks, twice as likely, to have a GED. Again, nativity differences exist. Among native-born Latino dropouts, more than one-in-five (21%) earned a GED, compared to just 5% of their foreign-born counterparts (Fry, 2010).

## CONCLUSION

While Latinos value a college education more than others, young Latinos are less likely to say they plan to get a college degree, and even fewer are enrolled in school. When asked why, most cite a need to support family as a reason for not continuing their education. Even so, young Latinos are optimistic. Almost three-in-four (72%) expect to be better off financially than their parents (Pew Hispanic Center, 2009).

The Great Recession, however, may have diminished young Latino's expectations about their financial futures and the benefits of a college education. According to an analysis of Current Population Survey data, in the fourth quarter of 2007, the unemployment rate among 25-to-34 year old Latino college graduates was 2.9%. By the fourth quarter of 2010, it was 8.1%. In comparison, among non-Hispanic White college graduates, the unemployment rate increased more modestly, from 1.8% in 2007 to 3.8% in 2010. But Latino college graduates did fare better during this recession compared with other Latinos. For example, among Latino high school graduates ages 25 to 34, the unemployment rate increased from 5.3% to 12.1% during the same period.

The 2010 decennial census counted 50.5 million Latinos in the United States, accounting for 16.3% of all Americans. Among the nation's children, Latinos are an even greater share: nearly 1 in 4 (23%) of those under age 18 are Latino (Passel, Cohn, & Lopez, 2011). By their numbers alone, how these young people come of age over the next few decades will determine what kind of nation America will be in this century.

## NOTES

1. I thank Rakesh Kochhar for many helpful discussions regarding this topic. I also thank him for providing unemployment estimates for Latinos by educational attainment.
2. The terms "foreign-born" and "immigrant" are used interchangeably throughout this chapter.

## REFERENCES

Fry, R. (2009, October). *The changing pathways of Hispanic youths into adulthood.* Washington, D.C.: Pew Hispanic Center.

Fry, R. (2010, May). *Hispanics, high school dropouts and the GED.* Washington, D.C.: Pew Hispanic Center.

Goldin, C., & Katz, L. F. (2007, March). *The race between education and technology: The evolution of U.S. educational wage differentials, 1890 to 2005.* Working paper 12984. Cambridge, MA: National Bureau of Economic Research.

Kewal Ramani, A., Gilbertson, L., Fox, M. A., & Provasnik, S. (2007, September). *Status and trends in the education of racial and ethnic minorities.* NCES 2007-039. Washington, D.C.: National Center for Education Statistics.

López, M. H. (2010, October). *Latinos and the 2010 elections: Strong support for Democrats; Weak voter motivation.* Washington, D.C.: Pew Hispanic Center.

López, M. H. (2009, October). *Latinos and education: Explaining the attainment gap.* Washington, D.C.: Pew Hispanic Center.

López, M. H., Morin, R., & Taylor, P. (2010, October). *Illegal immigration backlash worries, divides Latinos.* Washington, D.C.: Pew Hispanic Center.

U.S. Department of Education, National Center for Education Statistics. (2011, April). *Digest of Education Statistics 2010.* Washington, D.C.

Oreopoulos, P., & Salvanes, K. G. (2011). Priceless: The non-pecuniary benefits of schooling. *Journal of Economic Perspectives, 25*(1), 159–84.

Passel, J., Cohn, D., & Lopez, M. H. (2011, March). *Hispanics account for 56 percent of nation's growth in past decade; Census 2010: 50 million Hispanics.* Washington, D.C.: Pew Hispanic Center.

Pew Hispanic Center. (2009, December). *Between two worlds: How young Latinos come of age in America.* Washington, D.C.

Pew Hispanic Center. (2011, February). *Statistical portrait of Hispanics in the United States, 2009.* Washington, D.C.

Pew Research Center. (2010, February). *Millennials: A portrait of generation NEXT. Confident. Connected. Open to change.* Washington, D.C.

Schneider, B., Martinez, S., & Owens, A. (2006). Barriers to educational opportunities for Hispanics in the United States. In M. Tienda & F. Mitchell (Eds.), *Hispanics and the future of America.* Washington, D.C.: National Research Council.

Taylor, P., Parker, K., Fry, R., Cohn, D., Wang, W., Velasco, G., & Dockterman D. (2011, May). *Is college worth It? Surveys of college presidents and public assess value, quality and mission of higher education.* Washington, D.C.: Pew Social & Demographic Trends.

## APPENDIX

### 2009 National Survey of Latinos

The 2009 National Survey of Latinos from the Pew Hispanic Center, a project of the Pew Research Center, is a nationally representative telephone survey of 2,012 Hispanics ages 16 and older with an oversample of 1,240 Hispanics ages 16 to 25. The sample was randomly selected. Interviews were conducted on landline and cellular telephones from August 5, 2009 through September 16, 2009. The survey was conducted in English and Spanish. The margin of error for the full sample is plus or minus 3.7 percentage points at the 95% confidence level. For the youth sample, the margin of error is 4.6 percentage points.

### 2010 Millennial Survey

The 2010 Millennial Survey from the Pew Research Center is a nationally representative telephone survey of 2,020 adults ages 18 and older. The sample was randomly selected. Interviews were conducted January 14 to 27, 2010 on landline and cellular telephones. Interviews were conducted in English and Spanish. The sample includes an oversample of 830 respondents ages 18 to 29. The margin of error for the full sample is plus or minus 3 percentage points. For the youth sample, the margin of error is plus or minus 4 percentage points.

CHAPTER 3

# THE EVOLUTION OF HISPANIC LITERACY IN THE TWENTY-FIRST CENTURY

## From the First to the Third Generation

**Arturo Gonzalez**
*Office of the Comptroller of the Currency*

One particular on-going area of research considers whether the economic disparity between Hispanic immigrants and assimilated non-Hispanic Whites is narrowing or whether future generations of Hispanics will be part of a permanent underclass (e.g., Portes & Rumbaut, 1996; Trejo, 1997; Card, DiNardo, & Estes, 2000; Gonzalez, 2002; Borjas, 2006; Duncan & Trejo, 2007; Lazear, 2007). Extant research has mostly examined differences in earnings, occupation, and education between generations of Hispanics and non-Hispanics to examine whether or not assimilation is taking place.[1] One issue that has not received much attention by such assimilation studies is the literacy of Hispanics.

English-language literacy is an important component of Hispanic assimilation because immigrants with limited English-language ability represent a large fraction of Hispanics. The extent of the use of the English language

*The Economic Status of the Hispanic Population*, pages 33–48
Copyright © 2013 by Information Age Publishing
All rights of reproduction in any form reserved.

is backed by evidence that higher levels of English usage correlates with having attitudes and opinions similar to those of non-Hispanic Whites (Pew Hispanic Center, 2004). In addition to the use of the English language, the "type" or "quality" of English can be considered an important measure of assimilation. To function at a high level in American society, Hispanics (or any other group) must have excellent English-language writing and verbal skills—which in turn require a deep and well developed knowledge of English grammar, vocabulary, and the peculiarities of American English. Conversely, Hispanics unable to work with and understand printed and written information are at risk of not being able to gather and use information for their benefit, be it from a school pamphlet, a newspaper, or through the internet (U.S. Department of Education, 2007).

Multiple studies have noted the growing literacy requirements both in the workplace and society as a whole (U.S. Department of Education, 2001). For instance, it is well documented that Hispanics with lower English-language speaking ability earn less than similar workers who speak English only or very well (e.g., McManus, Gould, & Welch, 1983; McManus, 1985; Kossoudji, 1988; Gonzalez, 2000; Hamilton, Goldsmith, & Darity, 2008; Mora & Dávila, 2011). However, unlike English speaking ability, which is taken up by at least 95% of second- and third-generation Hispanics (Hakimzadeh & Cohn, 2007; Pew Hispanic Center, 2009), full assimilation in literacy may be more difficult to achieve by U.S.-born Hispanics because this skill requires higher levels of educational attainment than Hispanics are presently attaining (U.S. Department of Education, 2007; Lopez, 2009; Gonzalez, 2011). Therefore, the level of English-language literacy among Hispanics has a direct relationship on their earning potential.

At the same time, the low amount of English-language usage by Hispanic immigrants probably impacts the skill set of their U.S.-born children. Specifically, it is likely that second- and third-generation Hispanics have lower literacy levels because of the correlation of skills between generations that has been found for schooling and other outcomes (Borjas, 1992; Card et al., 2000; Leon, 2005).[2] While estimating the intergenerational assimilation effect for English-language literacy is beyond the scope of this chapter, examining differences in literacy by Hispanic and generation status provides a more nuanced assessment of how Hispanics are faring in the United States than is generally given. For example, the literature on the returns to education suggests that schooling quality might be a more appropriate measure than the number of school years (Behrman & Birdsall, 1983; Card & Krueger, 1992). Therefore, knowing whether Hispanics attain full assimilation with respect to English-language literacy is essential to assess their intergenerational mobility.

## THE NAAL SURVEY

Employing a unique survey—the 2003 National Assessment of Adult Literacy (NAAL)—this study examines differences in literacy in the English language between three generations of Hispanics and non-Hispanic Whites, and considers the effect of background factors in explaining such differences. The purpose of the NAAL was to obtain nationally representative measures of the English-language literacy of persons 16 and older. It gathered information on three types of literacy.

- *Prose literacy:* The knowledge and skills needed to search, comprehend, and use information from continuous texts, such as editorials, news stories, brochures, and instructional materials.
- *Document literacy:* The knowledge and skills needed to search, comprehend, and use information from non-continuous texts in various formats, including job applications, payroll forms, transportation schedules, maps, tables, and drug and food labels.
- *Quantitative literacy:* The knowledge and skills required to identify and perform computations, either alone or sequentially, using numbers embedded in printed materials, such as balancing a checkbook, figuring out a tip, completing an order form, and determining the amount of interest on a loan from an advertisement.

The final household NAAL sample consisted of about 18,100 persons. The derived scores for prose, document, and quantitative literacy range from 0 to 500, and can be interpreted using the following ranges (U.S. Department of Education, 2007):

|  | Prose | Document | Quantitative |
|---|---|---|---|
| Below Basic | 0–209 | 0–204 | 0–234 |
| Basic | 210–264 | 205–249 | 235–289 |
| Intermediate | 265–339 | 250–334 | 290–349 |
| Proficient | 340–500 | 335–500 | 350–500 |

## CHARACTERISTICS OF THE SAMPLE

The NAAL asked respondents to provide information about their place of birth, their parents' place of birth, as well as a host of other demographic characteristics. For the purposes of this study, the NAAL sample was restricted to Hispanics and non-Hispanic Whites living in households who had non-missing information on the characteristics included in the analysis.

The first generation is defined in this chapter as individuals who were not born in the United States and had two foreign-born parents. Note that persons born in the U.S. territories, including Puerto Rico, are classified here as foreign born. The second generation is defined as U.S.-born individuals who had one or two foreign-born parents. The third generation is defined as U.S.-born individuals who had two U.S.-born parents. This definition of the third generation includes fourth- and higher-generation respondents, and excludes persons born abroad of U.S. parents. The background characteristics included in the analysis are: language(s) learned before going to school, usual language(s) spoken now, how often the individual reads newspapers or books, age, years of education, school enrollment, gender, marital status, and census region of residence.

The demographic information from the NAAL survey shows that the Hispanic population was largely comprised of first- and second-generation Hispanics. Over 15 million Hispanics were foreign-born, which was nearly 60% of all Hispanics, compared to a share of 4% for non-Hispanic Whites. Furthermore, Hispanics outnumbered non-Hispanic Whites in the first-generation three to one. Second-generation Hispanics accounted for 23% of the Hispanic population, compared to nearly 10% for non-Hispanic Whites. Thus, less than one in five Hispanics (4.7 million) were third-generation Americans, accounting for less than 4% of the total third-generation population in 2003.

It is not surprising that the characteristics of the NAAL sample differed not just by Hispanic status, but also by generation status within the Hispanic population (full details are available from the author). In general, compared to non-Hispanic Whites, Hispanics were younger (33–38 years), more likely to be female, more likely to be enrolled in school, had completed fewer years of school, and were less likely to have ever married. Furthermore, Hispanics had fewer years of potential work experience,[3] were just as likely to have worked in the week before the survey, more likely to have a blue-collar job,[4] and earned less than $20,000 per year, compared to about $30,000 for non-Hispanic Whites. Hispanics were also more geographically concentrated than non-Hispanic Whites, with three-quarters living in the South and West. In contrast, about 45% of non-Hispanic Whites lived in the Midwest and Northeast at that time.

Several characteristics distinguish the first-generation Hispanics from other groups. First in terms of skills, the first generation averaged 10.1 years of school, 2.1–2.4 fewer years of schooling than second- and third-generation Hispanics. About 40% of first-generation Hispanics worked in blue-collar jobs, compared to less than 25% for every other group. This group also had the least amount of exposure to the U.S.-labor market (14 years compared to over 20 years for every other group). Half of Hispanic immigrants were men, slightly more than other U.S.-born groups, although non-Hispanic White immigrants were also more likely to be male.

Turning to more detailed examination of the NAAL respondents' literacy background reveals that whereas 75% and 98% of second- and third-generation non-Hispanic Whites learned only English before starting school, about 25% and 65% of Hispanics of the same generation did so. Instead, a large percentage of U.S.-born Hispanics were raised in a bilingual (about 22–36%) or Spanish-dominant household (14–38%). Despite these differences with non-Hispanic Whites, each succeeding generation of Hispanics was exposed to only English at home.

This pattern is similar in terms of languages spoken at home while growing up, except that a larger share of higher-generation Hispanics reported speaking both Spanish and English, 48–56%. Thus, although 65% of third-generation Hispanics reported learning to speak only English before school, 44% reported speaking only English at home while growing up. This lower number might reflect the open-ended nature of this question as opposed to the narrower period covered in the former question (i.e., "growing up" can be interpreted to include the teenage years, while "before school" implies an age of about six). Nevertheless, the survey reveals a decrease in the use of Spanish by Hispanics over the three generations: Spanish-only speakers made up 86% of the first generation, 30% of the second generation, but only 7% of the third generation.

Since the language that respondents were exposed to as children can affect the language outcomes in later years, the NAAL queried the language practices and self-reported ability of adults at the time of the survey. One such outcome is the language most often spoken. Hispanic adults of any generation were less likely than non-Hispanic Whites to be English-only speakers. Third-generation Hispanics were more likely than lower generations of Hispanics to speak only English, but at 61%, were still over 30 percentage points less likely than third-generation non-Hispanic Whites to speak only English.

The extent to which the language spoken by first-generation adults affected the likelihood that their children were English-only speakers (as adults) is not clear. Nevertheless, the fact that 33% of first-generation non-Hispanic Whites only spoke English, as opposed to 3% for Hispanics, raises the possibility that the outcomes observed in the second and third generations were linked to the literacy skill set of the first generation. Yet this does not mean that a large percentage of U.S.-born Hispanics did not speak English or become more literate in this language. For instance, the gap in English speaking between second-generation Hispanics and non-Hispanics Whites—64 percentage points—was almost twice as large as the gap for third-generation Hispanics (35 points). In fact, once bilingualism is considered, over 95% of second- and third-generation Hispanics reported usually speaking English.[5]

Self-reported English-language proficiency in speaking, understanding, reading, and writing are characteristics that provide insight into the English-language literacy background of Hispanics, although these may be imprecise and subjective measures. Respondents who reported being able to speak, understand, read, or write English "very well" or "well" are defined as proficient. Hispanics by far had the least self-reported English proficiency of the major racial/ethnic groups considered here. Less than half of Hispanic immigrants were not proficient in any of the four English-language skills (49% for speaking, 43% for understanding and reading, and 35% for writing), and the large size of the foreign-born population (60% of all Hispanics) shifted the average English proficiency levels of the overall Hispanic population downward.

Since English-language skills seemingly improve with time in the United States, the proficiency of subsequent generations of Hispanics should increase over time in the United States. Consistent with this expectation, the self-reported reading proficiency rates for second- and third-generation Hispanics was 93–94%, 94–97% for reading, 96–98% for understanding, and 97–99% for speaking. Thus, a significant amount of assimilation took place between the first and second generation with respect to acquiring English-language skills as reported by the respondents.

Finally, the NAAL asked respondents how frequently they read English-language books or newspapers/magazines. Although the answers to this question depended on the respondent's reading ability, not everyone who *can* read *will* read an English-language newspaper or a book. Still, it is not surprising that Hispanic immigrants were the least likely to say they read English-language books or newspapers/magazines, as between 26 and 36% reported reading either type of material at least a few times a week. In contrast, over half of non-Hispanic White immigrants read both types of printed media. Second- and third-generation Hispanics were also less likely to read either type of media than their non-Hispanic White counterparts. The biggest gap (eight percentage points) was for books and second-generation Hispanics (73% read English-language books); for newspapers and magazines, half of second- and third-generation Hispanics read newspapers, but were 4–5 percentage points less likely than non-Hispanic Whites to be involved in these English literacy activities.

## THREE MEASURES OF LITERACY IN THE NAAL

### Average Literacy Scores

While the information about literacy activities and background above is informative, the self-reported information is subjective and, thus, can be difficult to interpret. For instance, since nearly all U.S.-born Hispanics and non-Hispanic Whites said they can speak and understand the English language well or very well, this measure tells us little.

The NAAL provides three objective measures of English-language literacy which are comparable across groups. As seen in Table 3.1, the test-based measures of literacy reveal important differences between Hispanics (in Panel A) and non-Hispanics (in Panel B), regardless of which generation is considered. Consistent with the trends of the four self-reported English abilities discussed above, with average scores of 193, 182 and 209 for document, prose, and quantitative literacy, respectively, Hispanic immigrants

**TABLE 3.1   Means for Document, Prose and Quantitative English-Language Literacy, by Generation, in 2003**

| Ethnicity and Generation | Avg. Score | Below Basic | Basic | Inter-mediate | Proficient |
|---|---|---|---|---|---|
| **Panel A: Hispanics** | | | | | |
| *Document Literacy* | | | | | |
| First | 193.8 | 54.50% | 23.50% | 19.90% | 2.10% |
| Second | 263.1 | 11.00% | 27.30% | 56.20% | 5.50% |
| Third | 261.7 | 10.20% | 29.50% | 56.90% | 3.40% |
| *Prose Literacy* | | | | | |
| First | 182.2 | 67.10% | 21.40% | 10.40% | 1.20% |
| Second | 258.5 | 14.90% | 40.70% | 40.30% | 4.00% |
| Third | 269.0 | 9.10% | 38.60% | 47.10% | 5.10% |
| *Quantitative Literacy* | | | | | |
| First | 208.7 | 65.00% | 22.90% | 10.00% | 2.10% |
| Second | 259.0 | 32.20% | 39.20% | 25.30% | 3.30% |
| Third | 266.8 | 27.70% | 38.80% | 28.20% | 5.30% |
| **Panel B: Non-Hispanic Whites** | | | | | |
| *Document Literacy* | | | | | |
| First | 258.8 | 19.50% | 23.20% | 44.60% | 12.60% |
| Second | 267.8 | 12.00% | 23.70% | 55.00% | 9.30% |
| Third | 284.4 | 6.80% | 18.50% | 58.70% | 16.00% |
| *Prose Literacy* | | | | | |
| First | 255.0 | 25.30% | 29.50% | 35.50% | 9.70% |
| Second | 276.5 | 10.70% | 31.00% | 46.30% | 12.10% |
| Third | 291.0 | 6.40% | 24.10% | 52.30% | 17.20% |
| *Quantitative Literacy* | | | | | |
| First | 280.0 | 24.20% | 32.10% | 28.40% | 15.20% |
| Second | 281.6 | 21.30% | 34.20% | 32.50% | 12.00% |
| Third | 299 | 11.80% | 31.40% | 39.80% | 17.00% |

*Source:* Author's estimates using the 2003 NAAL; see text for sample selection.

*Notes:* Sample size is about 13,560 (rounded to the nearest 10 for confidentiality purposes). Maximum of 1,000 iterations used in the MML means procedure (described in this chapter's appendix). See text for cut-off points. Estimates are weighted and adjusted for strata and cluster effects.

had the lowest literacy levels of any group. Their scores were about 70 points lower than for first-generation non-Hispanic Whites; they were also 50–75 points less than for second- and third-generation Hispanics (259 [prose and quantitative], and 269 [prose] and 267 [quantitative], respectively). In contrast, the English-language literacy gap between first-generation non-Hispanic Whites and second- and third-generation Whites was at most 22 points. The average scores and distribution of the document, prose, and literacy scores based on the empirical model are described in further detail in the chapter appendix.

While the relatively low English literacy of Hispanic immigrants may be no surprise, the distributions of the test scores reveal that about 55–70% functioned at or below Basic English literacy level. This implies that a significant segment of the Hispanic immigrant population in 2003 had difficulties in locating identifiable information in prose text (e.g., not identifying from a pamphlet how often one should have a specified medical test), performing simple quantitative operations (e.g., calculating the price difference between two appliances from information in a table), or locating information and following instructions in simple documents (e.g., locating a phone number to call and get directions to a job fair) (U.S. Department of Education, 2007). At the other end of the English-language literacy distribution, less than three percent of Hispanic immigrants demonstrated English-language proficiency in any of these tasks.

Second- and third-generation Hispanics had significantly higher scores than Hispanic immigrants, but were still not on par with U.S.-born non-Hispanic Whites. Nevertheless, even as the average scores of third-generation Hispanics lagged behind non-Hispanic Whites, there was a clear pattern of increasing English-language literacy for Hispanics from the second to third generation. In fact, the average U.S.-born Hispanic demonstrated intermediate-level literacy (the low cut-off is 250) for document literacy. For prose literacy, only third-generation Hispanics were classified as Intermediate (52%), while for quantitative literacy, both generations of U.S.-born Hispanics fell in the Basic category. Thus, the three types of English-language literacy reveal progress among Hispanics over generations, but Hispanics still lagged behind their non-Hispanic White counterparts.

The information in Table 3.1 can be used to examine the extent of Hispanic assimilation, defined as convergence with third-generation non-Hispanic Whites, and calculated as the ratio of the average Hispanic score to the average third-generation White score for each English-language literacy type. By the second-generation, Hispanic document-English-language literacy trailed third-generation non-Hispanic Whites by 8%, and the gap was at least 8% for prose and quantitative literacy. However, the progress of assimilation with respect to English literacy was significantly slower from the second to the third generation. For document literacy, the gap between second-generation Hispanics and third-generations non-Hispanic Whites was not reduced. However, third-generation Hispanics reduced about 20 and 30% of the gap in quantitative and prose literacy, respectively. Thus, despite the slowing pace of assimilation, on average, third-generation Hispanics appear to have been catching up to third-generation non-Hispanic Whites. The next section considers whether differences in characteristics between Hispanics and third-generation non-Hispanic Whites accounted for these differences in English-language literacy.

## A More Detailed Analysis of Literacy Outcomes

The role of English-language background and demographic character-istics in English literacy outcomes is explored using a more rigorous em-pirical methodology, the details of which are provided in this chapter's appendix. Since Hispanics and non-Hispanics differ in demographic and language traits, and these traits have a direct impact on literacy (such as av-erage education), it is important to net out these separate effects. Table 3.2 shows the results for English-language literacy scores which are free of the impact of differences in characteristics. Column (1) considers how demo-graphic traits help reduce the gaps in literacy presented in Table 3.1, while Column (2) adds language characteristics and practices.

For instance, in Table 3.1, first-generation Hispanics had a gap of 90.5 points with third-generation non-Hispanic Whites in document English-language literacy; but after netting out demographic characteristics in Col-umn (I), the gap fell to 66.8 points (26% reduction in the literacy gap). The document literacy results for second- and third generation Hispanics (−18.9 and −21.5) imply that these gaps were 11 and 5% lower than the aver-age gaps in document literacy shown in Table 3.1.

The second column of each literacy type shows that accounting for differ-ences in English-language background between Hispanics and third-genera-tion non-Hispanic Whites further reduced the average gaps in literacy. After jointly considering differences in demographic and English-language traits, the average gap in the three literacy types fell by about 55% for Hispanic im-migrants, 37% for second-generation Hispanics, and 15–29% for third-gener-ation Hispanics. Thus, demographic and English-language background traits are important in accounting for the lower English literacy rates of Hispanics, but their importance differed for each generation of Hispanics.

Interestingly, although the English-language literacy variables measure different aspects of literacy, the results in Table 3.2 suggest that differences in characteristics were equally important in explaining the gap across dif-ferent types of literacy for each Hispanic generation. That is, the gap for each type of English-language literacy was reduced by a similar percent-

**TABLE 3.2  Empirical Results for the English-Language Literacy Outcomes for the Hispanic Generation Groups in 2003**

| Characteristic | Document (1) | Document (2) | Prose (1) | Prose (2) | Quantitative (1) | Quantitative (2) |
|---|---|---|---|---|---|---|
| Constant | 151.148 | 156.89 | 129.81 | 134.65 | 120.88 | 124.14 |
| | (4.23) | (4.21) | (5.32) | (5.17) | (5.30) | (5.33) |
| NH White×1st Generation | −25.50 | −14.58 | −36.66 | −19.63 | −21.58 | −9.69 |
| | (4.04) | (5.66) | (−3.57) | (4.48) | (3.72) | (5.37) |
| NH White×2nd Generation | −6.08 | −4.23 | −7.14 | −5.44 | −10.75 | −9.76 |
| | (2.69) | (2.58) | (2.21) | (2.39) | (2.64) | (2.52) |
| Hispanic×1st Generation | −66.78 | −40.39 | −79.44 | −48.16 | −62.49 | −41.30 |
| | (3.29) | (4.46) | (2.72) | (4.42) | (3.54) | (5.34) |
| Hispanic×2nd Generation | −18.85 | −13.34 | −26.94 | −20.42 | −30.35 | −24.79 |
| | (3.72) | (4.25) | (3.58) | (4.46) | (3.26) | (4.62) |
| Hispanic×3rd Generation | −21.46 | −19.22 | −18.26 | −15.92 | −24.91 | −22.70 |
| | (3.46) | (4.21) | (3.19) | (3.53) | (2.97) | (3.21) |
| Demographic traits | Yes | Yes | Yes | Yes | Yes | Yes |
| Language(s) learned before school; Language(s) usually spoken now; and Read English-language books or newspapers | No | Yes | No | Yes | No | Yes |

*Source:* Author's estimates using the 2003 NAAL.

*Notes:* Sample size is about 13,560 (rounded to the nearest 10 for confidentiality purposes). Demographic variables include age, age-squared, school years, enrolled in school interacted with school years, male, married or divorced or widowed, and region of resident. Estimates are weighted and adjusted for strata and cluster effects. See this chapter's appendix for more details.

age—55% for Hispanic immigrants, 37% for second-generation Hispanics, and 28% for third-generation Hispanics for prose and quantitative literacy. The exception is document literacy for third-generation Hispanics, which had the smallest reduction of all the results (−19.2 or 15% reduction of the average gap). Combined with the overall smaller impacts of background characteristics for third-generation Hispanics, this suggests that their English-language literacy outcomes require a more complex model and data to fully understand the reasons behind their lower literacy scores.

## CONCLUSION

This chapter used a survey to examine the English-language literacy of Hispanics in the United States by generation status in a more detailed manner than previous studies. In addition to several objective-based measures of literacy, this study differentiates between three (cross-sectional) generations of Hispanics. The results show that the gap in document, prose, and quantitative literacy scores between Hispanics and third-generation non-Hispanic Whites in 2003 was reduced by succeeding generations of Hispanics. This is especially noticeable from the first to the second generation for all three types of literacy. Although the extent of assimilation with respect to English-language literacy decreased from the second to the third generation, third-generation Hispanics had higher literacy scores and smaller gaps with third-generation non-Hispanic Whites than second-generation Hispanics.

Demographic and English-language characteristics are correlated with the English-language literacy gap between Hispanics and third-generation non-Hispanic Whites. Both types of characteristics helped to explain the lower English literacy of Hispanics and should be jointly considered in future analyses. This was especially true for first- and second-generation Hispanics, and less so for third-generation Hispanics. The English-language literacy outcomes of third-generation Hispanics is not as well explained in this study, and therefore requires a more complex study.

Since third-generation non-Hispanic Whites were probably more assimilated in general than third-generation Hispanics (because a larger share of "third-generation" non-Hispanic Whites in this category was in fact fourth- and higher generation), it is likely that third-generation Hispanics will continue to reduce the English-language literacy gap with succeeding generations.[6] While the empirical analysis was limited to a cross-sectional generational study, the results suggest that added exposure to, and use of, the English language during childhood and as adults are likely to fuel further assimilation with respect to English-language literacy for Hispanics. The same is true for the increases in educational attainment.

The results of this chapter provide evidence that Hispanics are making progress in English-language literacy, but the results suggest certain policy opportunities for policymakers. First, it is important to continue gathering data on literacy. However, to provide more definitive analyses across generations, it would be worthwhile to collect more detailed information about generation status and/or gather longitudinal data. This would improve the comparability between Hispanic and non-Hispanic White populations. Second, expanding the availability of English-language courses to Hispanic immigrants could also enhance their children's exposure to English at home.

In addition to literacy tasks, the NAAL contains information about the respondent's language background, including English-language ability in speaking, understanding, reading, and writing, as well as language-use activities. Even when states face budget challenges, it is important that policymakers consider the intergenerational benefits of these programs in their cost-benefit assessment of these programs (Gonzalez, 2007). Another policy implication from these results is the importance of expanding the educational and intellectual achievement for parents and their children. This not only includes further gains in college enrollment and graduation, but also programs at schools and in the home that promote literacy activities, such as reading for leisure. While failure to implement such policies is unlikely to stunt further gains in literacy for Hispanics in both absolute and relative terms, implementing such policies may speed up the assimilation process with respect to English-language literacy.

*Disclaimer.* The opinions expressed in this chapter are those of the author, and do not necessarily reflect the views of the Office of the Comptroller of the Currency or the Department of the Treasury.

## NOTES

1. Studies tend to find that, on average, third-generation Hispanics have not fully caught up with third-generation non-Hispanic Whites, but it is not clear whether their progress has stalled or will continue into future generations. It should be pointed out that most studies, including this one, rely on cross-sectional data rather than longitudinal data, and hence the results are based on an imperfect comparison of "generations." Duncan and Trejo (2007) find evidence that persons of Mexican-descent are less likely to identify as such as part of the assimilation process. If this is the case, measures of assimilation are biased towards finding lower levels of assimilation.

2. The impact, $b$, one generation's skill set has on the skill level of the next generation is called the "intergenerational assimilation rate." For schooling, the assimilation rate, $1 - b$, between the first- and second-generation is about 0.70, meaning that about 70% of the gap between the first-generation and the population average is closed by the second generation (Borjas, 1992; Card et al., 2000).

3. Potential work experience is calculated as Age − (School Years + 6) for those not enrolled in school. For immigrants whose (Age at Arrival) exceeds (School Years + 6), potential work experience is Years in the United States, defined as Age − (Age at Arrival).

4. Blue collar occupations include farm, construction, production, transportation, and installation occupations. White collar occupations include professional, management, and service occupations.

5. The fact that Hispanics also tend to speak Spanish may be a benefit, as bilingualism can open up job opportunities not necessarily available to monolingual English speakers. Studies tend not to find a positive correlation between bilingualism and wages (Fry & Lowell, 2003; Cortina, de la Garza, & Pinto, 2007). This could be due to a large supply of native-Spanish speakers concentrated in particular labor markets, or combining Hispanics of different generations into one group, or ability and self-selection bias. Saiz and Zoido (2005) consider foreign-language skills acquired by American college students and find a 2–3% return, perhaps reflecting the importance of differentiating language skills that are acquired with little costs (such as by native speakers) and those with high costs (such by non-native speakers in college).

6. This assumes that third- and higher generations Hispanics continue to self-identify as Hispanics to be able to study them (Duncan & Trejo, 2007).

## APPENDIX

Every respondent in the NAAL was given a literacy assessment booklet containing seven core tasks plus three blocks of literacy tasks (each block contained approximately 11 questions). The respondents were not given the same three blocks of literacy tasks, however; as answering all 152 literacy tasks (core questions + 12 blocks of tasks) would have taken more than three hours. In order to balance time constraint and coverage of literacy tasks, respondents were given one of 26 configurations of three blocks of tasks. The assignment of particular three blocks of tasks was based on a balanced incomplete block (BIB) spiraling design. Under the BIB design, approximately 11 questions were placed into a block, and three blocks were assigned to assessment booklets in a systematic way. In particular, the blocks were spiraled so that each block was paired with every other block across the 26 different configurations of the assessment booklet, and each block appeared in each of the three positions (first, middle, last) in a booklet (U.S. Department of Education, 2009). This design has the benefit of reducing the time commitment of each respondent, while also increasing the number of literacy tasks that can be assigned, ensuring that underlying literacy trait is fully covered by the tasks.

Using a BIB spiraling design approach makes it possible to obtain unbiased estimates of literacy scores for populations without first obtaining accurate estimates for individuals. Using "item response theory," marginal maximum likelihood (MML) regression is used to derive unbiased estimates of proficiency scales. This MML regression procedure estimates a linear regression for data in which the dependent variable (e.g., responses to a subtest of questions) is only partially observed. MML regression makes it possible to link responses from the different booklets to a common scale by representing a respondent's score by a probability distribution over all of possible scores of the literacy being measured. Thus, MML regression provides parameter estimates of literacy for a population rather than for individuals.

For the empirical study, proficiency in English, $y$, is modeled as a linear function of binary variables indicating Hispanic × U.S. generation ($HG$) status, binary variables indicating language-spoken before school ($L1$), present English-language practices ($L2$), demographic variables ($X$), and an error term ($\varepsilon$) assumed to have a normal distribution:

$$y_i = c_i + HG_i\delta + L1_i\beta_1 + L2_i\beta_2 + X_i\beta_3 + \varepsilon_i$$

Specifically the binary variables of *HG* are first-generation non-Hispanic White, second-generation non-Hispanic White, first-generation Hispanic, second-generation Hispanic, and third-generation Hispanic, with third-generation non-Hispanic White as the omitted category; the *L1* variables include language(s) spoken before school, with English-only the omitted category; the *L2* variables are language(s) used in speaking and reading and how often respondent reads newspapers or books in English; and the demographic characteristics are age, age-squared, completed years of school, interaction of school enrollment and school years, male, marital status, and region of residence. School enrollment is interacted with years of school since the years of school for NAAL student respondents are not comparable to those who have left school (especially for those under 25 years old).

Since proficiency for each respondent is measured as a subset of the 152 available tasks and is therefore not directly observed, ordinary least squares regression cannot be used with these data. Instead of the same dependent variable for each respondent, each respondent has a different dependent variable because respondents received one of the 26 assessment booklets. For this reason, the dependent variable is instead represented as a probability distribution of proficiency through a likelihood function. This likelihood function is estimated using MML models. The regression analysis incorporates the survey design weight, cluster and strata variables of the NAAL survey. Separate MML regressions are carried out for each literacy type and for different sets of control variables. For further details regarding MML see U.S. Department of Education (2009). The MML Regression procedure with 1000 maximum iterations is estimated using the "AM" statistical software developed by American Institutes for Research for use with the NAAL. Full estimates are available upon request from the author.

## REFERENCES

Behrman, J. R., & Birdsall, N. (1983). The quality of schooling: Quantity alone is misleading. *American Economic Review, 73*(5), 928–946.

Borjas, G. J. (1982). The labor supply of male Hispanic immigrants in the United States. *International Migration Review, 17*(4), 343–353.

Borjas, G. J. (1992). Ethnic capital and intergenerational mobility. *Quarterly Journal of Economics, 107*(1), 123–150.

Borjas, G. J. (2006). Making it in America: Social mobility in the immigrant population. Working Paper 12088. National Bureau of Economic Research. Cambridge, MA.

Card, D., DiNardo, J., & Estes, E. (2000). The more things change: Immigrants and the children of immigrants in the 1940s, the 1970s, and the 1990s. In G. J. Borjas (Ed.), *Issues in the economics of immigration* (pp. 227–269). Chicago, IL: University of Chicago Press.

Card, D., & Krueger, A. B. (1992). Does school quality matter? Returns to education and the characteristics of public schools in the United States. *The Journal of Political Economy, 100*(1), 1–40.

Cortina, J., de la Garza, R. O., & Pinto, P. M. (2007). *No entiendo*: The effects of bilingualism on Hispanic earnings. Working Paper 2007–03. Institute for Social and Economic Research and Policy. New York.

Duncan, B., & Trejo, S. J. (2007). Ethnic identification, intermarriage, and unmeasured progress by Mexican Americans. In G. J. Borjas (Ed.), *Mexican immigration to the United States* (pp. 229–267). Chicago: University of Chicago Press.

Fry, R., & Lowell, B. L. (2003). The value of bilingualism in the U.S. labor market. *Industrial and Labor Relations Review, 57*(1), 128–140.

Gonzalez, A. (2000). The acquisition and labor market value of four English skills: New evidence from NALS. *Contemporary Economic Policy, 18*(3), 259–269.

Gonzalez, A. (2002). *Mexican Americans & the U.S. economy: Quest for buenos días.* Tucson, AZ: University of Arizona Press.

Gonzalez, A. (2007). *California's commitment to adult English learners: Caught between funding and need.* Public Policy Institute of California. San Francisco, CA.

Gonzalez, A. (2011). Hispanic and first-generation college students: How do they fare in postsecondary education? In S. J. Trejo & D. Leal (Eds.), *Latinos and the economy: Integration and impact in schools, labor markets, and beyond* (pp. 95–112). New York: Springer.

Hakimzadeh, S., & Cohn, D. (2007). *English usage among Hispanics in the United States.* Pew Hispanic Center. Washington, D.C.

Hamilton, D., Goldsmith, A. H., & Darity, W. J. (2008). Measuring the wage costs of limited English: Issues with using interviewer versus self-reports in determining Latino wages. *Hispanic Journal of Behavioral Sciences, 30*(3), 257–279.

Kossoudji, S. A. (1988). English language ability and the labor market opportunities of Hispanic and east Asian immigrant men. *Journal of Labor Economics, 6*(2), 205–228.

Lazear, E. P. (2007). Mexican assimilation in the United States. In G. J. Borjas (Ed.), *Mexican immigration to the United States* (pp. 107 –121). Chicago, IL: The University of Chicago Press.

Leon, A. (2005). *Does "ethnic capital" matter? Identifying peer effects in the intergenerational transmission of ethnic differentials.* University of Pittsburgh. Pittsburgh, PA.

Lopez, M. H. (2009). *Latinos and education: Explaining the education gap.* Pew Hispanic Center. Washington, D.C.

McManus, W. S. (1985). Labor market costs of language disparity: An interpretation of Hispanic earnings differences. *American Economic Review, 75*(4), 818–827.

McManus, W. S., Gould, W., & Welch, F. (1983). Earnings of Hispanic men: The role of English language proficiency. *Journal of Labor Economics, 1*(2), 101–130.

Mora, M. T., & Davila, A. (2011). The LEP earnings penalty among Hispanic men in the U.S. : 1980–2005. In S. J. Trejo & D. Leal (Eds.), *Latinos and the economy: Integration and impact in schools, labor markets, and beyond* (pp. 153–167). New York: Springer.

Pew Hispanic Center (2004). *Assimilation and language.* Pew Hispanic Center. Washington, D.C.

Pew Hispanic Center (2009). *Between two worlds: How young Latinos come of age in America.* Pew Hispanic Center. Washington, D.C.

Portes, A., & Rumbaut, R. G. (1996). *Immigrant America: A portrait* (2nd Ed.). Berkeley: University of California Press.

Saiz, A., & Zoido, E. (2005). Listening to what the world says: Bilingualism and earnings in the United States. *Review of Economics and Statistics, 87*(3), 523–538.

Trejo, S. J. (1997). Why do Mexican Americans earn low wages? *Journal of Political Economy, 105*(6), 1235–1268.

U.S. Department of Education, NCES (2001). *Adult literacy and education in America: Four studies based on the National Adult Literacy Survey* (NCES 1999–469). Washington, D.C.

U.S. Department of Education, NCES (2007). *Literacy in everyday life: Results from the 2003 National Assessment of Adult Literacy* (NCES 2007–480). Washington, D.C.

U.S. Department of Education, NCES (2009). *Technical report and data file user's manual for the 2003 National Assessment of Adult Literacy* (NCES 2009–476). Washington, D.C.: U.S. GPO.

CHAPTER 4

# POVERTY AMONG HISPANICS IN THE UNITED STATES

**Mary J. Lopez**
*Occidental College*

In 2010, according to the United States Census Bureau, among the over 46 million people living in poverty in the United States, approximately 13.2 million (29%) were Hispanic, making them the racial/ethnic minority group most respiresented among the poor. This said, economic growth, expanded income support policies, and efforts to eliminate explicit discriminatory practices contributed to falling poverty rates and a narrowing of the racial and ethnic gaps in poverty before the Great Recession (Cancian & Danziger, 2009). However, large disparities in poverty have persisted, even after the Great Recession that struck a devastating blow to the U.S. labor market, as Hispanics and Blacks were twice as likely to be poor as non-Hispanic Whites in 2010. Understanding why racial and ethnic disparities continue to persist is important in mitigating poverty among Hispanic and Black Americans.

Several factors may be associated with the persistent racial and ethnic disparities in poverty. First, labor market opportunities differ across racial and ethnic groups. In 2000, for example, Hispanics comprised 44.2% of the workforce with less than a high school diploma (Borjas, 2006). At the

*The Economic Status of the Hispanic Population*, pages 49–64
Copyright © 2013 by Information Age Publishing
All rights of reproduction in any form reserved.

same time, increasing returns to education and rising income inequality resulted in weak labor market outcomes for high school dropouts relative to college educated workers. Thus, racial and ethnic differences in earnings and employment opportunities can contribute to racial poverty disparities. Second, individual choices about investments in human capital, labor force participation, and family formation may differ across racial and ethnic groups. For example, Dennis Sullivan and Andrea Ziegert (2008) found that poverty among Hispanic immigrants mainly results from their low levels of education and a lack of fluency in the English language. In addition, Hispanics may exhibit high poverty rates because, according to a 2008 Pew Hispanic Center report, they are more likely than any other racial group to live in households with five or more persons.

Third, structural factors shape the choices available to individuals and may differ by race and ethnicity (Cancian & Danziger, 2009). For example, housing discrimination against racial minorities may result in residential segregation and disparities in educational and labor market opportunities. Finally, immigration may contribute to poverty. George Borjas (2006) has argued the large scale immigration altered the racial and ethnic composition of the disadvantaged workforce. A greater representation of Hispanics among low-wage, less educated workers makes Hispanics more vulnerable to poverty.

## WHAT EXPLAINS RACIAL AND ETHNIC POVERTY GAPS?

In evaluating the factors contributing to racial and ethnic poverty gaps, it is important to begin by recognizing that the poor are not a homogeneous group (Simms, 2009). For example, according to the Census Bureau, 34.2% of all single, female-headed households lived in poverty in 2010. As with poverty rates in general, the rates vary by race and ethnicity, as over 40% of all Hispanic and Black single, female-headed households resided below the poverty line in 2010, compared to 24.8% for non-Hispanic Whites. The diversity among the poor can also be found within a single racial-ethnic group; indeed, there is a significant amount of heterogeneity among the Hispanic population living in poverty by country of origin and nativity status. For example, the Pew Hispanic Center reports that in 2009, Hondurans had a poverty rate of 27% compared to 24% for Mexican Americans and 12% for Colombians.

### Labor Market Outcomes

The macroeconomy, earnings and employment, and income inequality are important factors that contribute to poverty. As discussed by Maria Cancian and Sheldon Danziger, between 1973 and 1993, the Hispanic poverty rate increased from 21.9% to 30.6%, representing the largest increase in poverty among all racial-ethnic groups in the United States over the 20-year period. This surge is partly attributed to the worsening wage and employment outcomes for less educated workers relative to college graduates. The large and growing concentration of Hispanics in the low-skill workforce makes this group particularly vulnerable to poor labor market outcomes and long-term poverty spells. Cancian and Danziger reported that after 1993, the negative trend reversed, as tight labor markets and rising real wages for less-educated workers contributed to dramatic *decreases* in the poverty rates for minorities. By the turn of the century, the poverty rate had fallen to 21.5% for Hispanics. Richard Freeman (2001) also showed that the rising real wages and employment opportunities in the 1990s reduced poverty rates, particularly among Hispanics and Blacks.

In a tight labor market, firms have a greater difficulty meeting employment needs and can respond by increasing wages or by providing training and job opportunities to individuals who might not otherwise meet the desired job qualifications (Blank, 2000). The underemployed, who constitute discouraged and involuntary part-time workers, benefit as employment grows. For example, the booming construction industry contributed to the strong employment gains among Hispanics during the period prior to the Great Recession. While racial-ethnic minorities can benefit from economic booms, they tend to be disproportionately affected during economic recessions, as they comprise a large segment of the low-skill workforce and have less savings and wealth to use as a cushion. For example, between 2007 and 2008, the downturn in the construction industry erased the employment gains that Hispanics realized prior to the recession (Kochhar, 2008). In addition, since earnings growth can fall behind employment, the wages of racial-ethnic minorities will likely continue to lag behind those of non-Hispanics.

Rising income inequality represents another contributing factor to poverty. Richard Freeman (2001) discussed how the weakening of the relationship between economic growth and poverty can be partly attributed to the rise in wage inequality. If the earnings distribution is stable and real wages rise, then poverty should decrease with economic growth. However, Freeman argues that as income inequality rises, the shape of the income distribution changes, which can offset any effects of growth on poverty. In the 1980s, the real wages of less skilled workers declined while those of skilled workers increased, thus widening the distribution of wages. As a result, poverty rates increased, particularly for Hispanics and Blacks. Similarly, John Iceland (2003) reported that the increasing income inequality between 1969 and 1990 was associated with an increase in the poverty rates for all racial and ethnic groups, but that the effect was greatest among Hispanics, partly as a result of their concentration in low-skill occupations.

Empirical evidence has shown that labor market variables can have an important impact on poverty. Analyzing aggregate poverty rates from 1967 to 2003, Hilary Hoynes, Marianne Page, and Ann Huff Stevens (2006) estimated that a one percentage-point increase in the unemployment rate increased the poverty rate by 0.5 percentage points, a 10% increase in the median wage reduced the poverty rate by 1.5 percentage points, and a 10% increase in income inequality increased the poverty rate by 2.5 percentage points. However, the authors reported that the predictive power of these labor market variables in explaining poverty weakened over time. Rebecca Blank (2009) similarly showed that the link between poverty and the unemployment rate weakened in the 1980s, only to strengthen during the 1990–2006 period. Analyzing regional data, Timothy Bartik (2001) found that a strong overall economy has a significant effect in lowering poverty, but this effect slightly fell in the 1980s.

While growth in earnings and employment opportunities matter for mitigating poverty, economic growth alone is not enough to eliminate racial and poverty differentials. Freeman showed that a substantial number of individuals living in poverty in 1999 had characteristics that made it difficult for them to benefit from a booming economy, such as low labor force participation rates, low educational attainment, and high disability rates. As a result, such individuals become vulnerable to economic downturns.

## Individual Choices

A second theory for the persistence of poverty pertains to choice-based behavior. Individuals are poor not because of structural societal conditions, but as a result of their choices about investments in human capital, labor force participation, or family formation. This particular theory assumes that individuals make decisions which subsequently affect their socioeconomic outcomes. For example, an individual can freely choose from among several different schooling levels or the number of hours to work, the consequences of which affect their labor market income. As such, an alternative choice existed that might have provided a greater economic opportunity, but the individual chose not to select that option (Blank, 2003).

Analyzing 2007 Current Population Survey data, Daniel Meyer and Geoffrey Wallace (2009) showed that human capital, work effort, and family formation closely relate to poverty. Poverty rates for families in which the household head had less than a high school diploma were twice as high as those in which the head had a high school diploma. Female-headed households and households with six or more people also had high poverty rates. Only 4.2% of individuals working full-year/full-time were poor compared to 24.3% of other individuals. The authors also indicated that some individuals have certain characteristics that make them more vulnerable to poverty. For example, female household heads with low levels of education had predicted poverty rates of 51%.

Criminal behavior can further contribute to poverty. Cancian and Danziger (2009) noted that individuals who had been incarcerated face limited employment prospects. Incarcerated individuals may also have a difficult time obtaining student financial aid or housing assistance (Wheelock & Uggen, 2008). Steven Raphael (2007) showed that Hispanics were more likely to be incarcerated than non-Hispanic Whites, as 7.7% of Hispanic men had served time in prison compared to 2.6% for non-Hispanic Whites in 2001.

Choice theory can be used to explain intergenerational poverty if preferences are passed on from one generation to the next. Based on this theory, the correct policy response would be to encourage people to behave differently through positive support or sanctions (Blank, 2003). For example, the 1996 Welfare Reform required recipients to participate in work or work related activities and it established a time limit on aid.

For racial/ethnic disparities in poverty to exist as a result of individual choice, one must believe that individual behavior differs across groups. Thus, while Hispanics have lower levels of schooling compared to non-Hispanic Whites, it is not clear this solely stems from differences in individual behavior among members of the two groups. An alternative explanation involves how group characteristics predict individual behavior (Durlauf, 2001); individual decisions about human capital, labor force participation, or family formation are guided by the groups in which individuals belong during their lifetimes. However, it may be the case that racial-ethnic disparities in poverty stem from the structural factors that shape the set of choices available to an individual. Meyer and Wallace (2009) predicted the poverty rate for non-Hispanic Whites with low levels of education to be 26.7%, compared to 38.4% for non-Whites. Thus, holding education and other characteristics constant, the predicted poverty rates of racial minorities were disproportionately high.

## Structural Factors that Shape Choices

John Yinger (2001) suggested several explanations for how the housing market can contribute to poverty. First, high rents form barriers for poor individuals to invest in human capital and health care. Second, poor quality housing can contribute to reduced health conditions, which again prevent individuals from investing in human capital. Third, barriers to homeownership (such as credit constraints) prevent individuals from gaining access to wealth, which can be used as a buffer during economic downturns or during an illness. Finally, housing markets may not adjust to the movement of low-skill jobs to the suburbs, resulting in a mismatch between residential locations and job locations. If so, low-skilled workers may not be able to relocate to areas with employment growth. Yinger further argued that housing markets may maintain racial and ethnic poverty disparities as a result of discrimination. For example, housing discrimination has contributed to racial residential segregation which ultimately shapes the set of choices available to individuals (Cancian & Danziger, 2009). Thus, the structure of the housing market and the continued evidence of discrimination in the housing market contribute to racial/ethnic poverty disparities.

Another possible structural factor contributing to poverty is the criminal justice system. Cancian and Danziger (2009) argued that while racial and ethnic differences in incarceration rates reflect differences in criminal behavior, they also reflect racial/ethnic variations in treatment by the criminal justice system. For example, analyzing sentencing data for Pennsylvania, Darrell Steffensmeier and Stephen Demuth (2001) reported that Hispanics received the harshest penalties for drug and non-drug cases. When prisoners are released from prison they often face labor market discrimination and other restrictions that can perpetuate poverty. For example, Darren Wheelock and Christopher Uggen (2008) noted that New York and Florida prohibit previously incarcerated individuals from low-skilled occupations such as taxi drivers, junk dealers, and farm laborers. Moreover, these authors note that previously incarcerated individuals are ineligible for federal college loans and grants, welfare assistance, public housing, and military benefits. Devah Pager (2003) further showed that previously incarcerated individuals were less likely to be called back when they submitted job applications. Thus, eliminating racial/ethnic disparities in poverty may require changes to our institutional structures and policies.

## Immigration

George Borjas (2006) has argued that the increase in the Hispanic foreign-born population explains a large part of the decline in the economic status of Hispanics relative to other racial and ethnic groups. Hispanics represented 13.8% of the high-school-dropout workforce (7% U.S.-born Hispanics and 6.8% Hispanic immigrants) in 1980, but by 2000, their representation in this workforce increased to 44.2% (8.4% U.S.-born Hispanics and 35.8% Hispanic immigrants). During the same time, Borjas estimated that the male Hispanic/non-Hispanic wage differential widened in magnitude from 30% to 45%.

Nevertheless, while Steven Raphael and Eugene Smolensky (2009) reported that poverty rates among immigrants in the United States increased between 1970 and 2005, they found only modest effects of immigration on poverty among Hispanics overall. Hoynes, Page, and Huff Stevens also uncovered little evidence that immigration significantly contributed to higher poverty levels. While immigration might further contribute to rising poverty rates if immigrants compete with U.S.-born workers (thus lowering their wage and employment outcomes), Raphael and Smolensky estimated little impact of greater immigrant-native labor market competition on poverty rates.

The different theories behind factors affecting the incidence of poverty can be difficult to empirically test. As such, the analysis below does not provide empirical evidence for all of the poverty theories previously discussed for Hispanics and other groups, but it attempts to identify some of the main factors that influence the likelihood of residing below the poverty line. It also sheds light on how these poverty determinants differ between Hispanics and non-Hispanic Whites as well as across various Hispanic subgroups.

## BASIC TRENDS IN POVERTY

The data used to analyze poverty rates of Hispanics are from the 1990 and 2000 U.S. decennial censuses and the 2006–2008 three-year sample of the American Community Survey (ACS), as provided by the Integrated Public Use Microdata Series at the Minnesota Population Center (Ruggles et al., 2010), and described in the Data Appendix chapter. The sample is restricted to all household heads between the ages of 18 and 64 and excludes those living in group quarters and those currently enrolled in school. The household heads are all unrelated and thus comprise a sample of primary families and primary individuals.[1]

Poverty rates (defined as the share of individuals whose family incomes fall below the federally established poverty thresholds) by race and ethnicity reveal large differences between non-Hispanic Whites and other racial minority groups.[2] However, as discussed above, even racial-ethnic poverty rates mask important differences by age, gender, nativity, and ethnic-origin groups. To highlight such differences, Table 4.1 displays the poverty rates among household heads by gender, nativity status, and Hispanic-origin between 1990 and 2008. The data reveal several interesting trends. First, while gender-related poverty gaps have narrowed over time (partly as a result of the narrowing gender wage gap in the United States and a greater participation of women in the labor force), women continued to exhibit higher poverty rates than men in 2006–2008. In addition, these gender poverty gaps differed across groups. For example, as seen in Panel A, this gap was largest among non-Hispanic Whites (12.3% among women vs. 5.8% among men) and smallest among Asians (11.5% vs. 6.4%). Within

**TABLE 4.1   Poverty Rates of Household Heads by Gender, Hispanic Origin, and Nativity: 1990–2008**

| Characteristic | 1990 | | 2000 | | 2006–2008 | |
|---|---|---|---|---|---|---|
| | Men | Women | Men | Women | Men | Women |
| Panel A: Race/ethnicity | | | | | | |
| Non-Hispanic Whites | 5.1% | 16.1% | 5.0% | 13.8% | 5.8% | 12.3% |
| Hispanics | 15.9% | 38.2% | 15.7% | 31.9% | 13.8% | 27.4% |
| Blacks | 14.2% | 38.8% | 13.6% | 31.3% | 14.4% | 28.5% |
| Asians | 7.8% | 18.1% | 7.9% | 16.2% | 6.4% | 11.5% |
| Panel B: Hispanic subgroups | | | | | | |
| Mexican | 18.2% | 38.2% | 17.2% | 32.0% | 15.5% | 29.2% |
| Puerto Rican | 14.2% | 48.6% | 14.1% | 38.2% | 13.3% | 31.9% |
| Cuban | 8.9% | 24.0% | 10.3% | 20.2% | 8.5% | 16.6% |
| Dominican | 16.7% | 47.4% | 16.4% | 39.4% | 13.4% | 33.0% |
| Other Central American | 16.5% | 32.3% | 14.8% | 28.4% | 11.8% | 24.3% |
| South American | 8.4% | 23.0% | 9.8% | 21.9% | 7.7% | 14.8% |
| Other | 6.8% | 20.6% | 7.1% | 16.9% | 7.1% | 16.0% |
| Panel C: Nativity | | | | | | |
| Foreign-born Whites | 5.1% | 16.2% | 4.9% | 13.8% | 5.7% | 12.3% |
| U.S.-born Whites | 6.3% | 13.9% | 7.8% | 14.4% | 7.3% | 11.5% |
| Foreign-born Hispanics | 19.1% | 36.7% | 18.5% | 33.7% | 15.9% | 30.4% |
| U.S.-born Hispanics | 12.9% | 39.1% | 11.5% | 30.5% | 10.5% | 24.6% |
| Foreign-born Blacks | 14.4% | 39.5% | 13.8% | 32.0% | 15.0% | 29.4% |
| U.S.-born Blacks | 10.6% | 21.1% | 11.4% | 21.4% | 9.8% | 17.9% |
| Foreign-born Asians | 3.7% | 12.1% | 5.2% | 13.1% | 4.9% | 9.6% |
| U.S.-born Asians | 8.8% | 20.2% | 8.5% | 17.1% | 6.7% | 12.0% |

*Notes:* Author's calculations based on the 1990 and 2000 U.S. Censuses and the 2006–2008 American Community Surveys. The samples are restricted to household heads between the ages of 18–64 who did not reside in group quarters.

the Hispanic population (Panel B), in 2006–08 Mexican Americans (the largest Hispanic subgroup) had the smallest gender poverty gap in relative terms (29.2% vs. 15.5%), while Dominicans (the fifth largest group) had the widest gap (33.0% vs. 13.3%) of the groups shown. Turning to nativity (Panel C), immigrants tended to have higher poverty rates than U.S.-born household heads, with some exceptions (notably Asians). In fact, foreign-born Asian men had the lowest poverty rates in the three time periods of all the groups listed in Table 4.1.

Among the foreign-born, Hispanic men and women had the highest poverty rates of the groups shown in 2000 and 2006–08. These gaps may partly reflect differences in U.S.-specific human capital, such as proficiency in the English language. Finally, while poverty rates have fallen over time for all Hispanic subgroups, considerable variation continued to exist. For example, Mexican American men had the highest poverty rate (15.5%) among men, and Dominicans had the highest rate (33.0%) among women in 2006–2008. Thus, while Hispanics were more likely to reside below the poverty line than non-Hispanic Whites, Table 4.1 shows that Hispanic women and the foreign-born were even more vulnerable to poverty.

The previous section in this chapter provided several different explanations for disparities in poverty rates across racial and ethnic groups. Consistent with economic theory, a closer examination of the 2006 versus 08 data (details available from the author) reveals that, in terms of labor market outcomes, impoverished household heads had lower earnings, employment rates, and labor force participation rates than their non-impoverished counterparts. For example, 70% of Hispanic men living in poverty were employed compared to 91% of other Hispanic men during this time. This gap was even wider for Hispanic women, as only 42% of impoverished Hispanic women had jobs compared to 77% of other Hispanic women. The poor were also less likely to work full-year/full-time. For example, among Hispanic men living in poverty, 42% worked full-year/full-time, about half the share (81%) observed for non-impoverished Hispanic men.

Differences in human capital are evident. To illustrate, poor household heads had fewer years of schooling than other household heads. For example, Hispanic men and women residing above the poverty line in 2006–08 had 11.7 and 12.3 schooling years, respectively, compared to their impoverished counterparts, who had 9.6 and 10.3 years. English-language proficiency (defined as those individuals who speak English at least "well") was also lower among poor versus non-poor Hispanics, which related to the disproportionate share of the foreign-born among the poor. To illustrate, immigrants represented 71.2% of Hispanic men, and 55.3% of Hispanic women, living in poverty in 2006–08, compared to 60.1% and 47.7% of other Hispanic men and women.

Decisions about family formation may further contribute to poverty. Having a larger family is generally observed among Hispanics. With the exception of non-Hispanic White men, the poor had more children on average than the non-poor. In addition, the poor were more likely to be single heads of household.

These patterns provide supportive evidence for several of the poverty explanations, and they demonstrate why disparities may arise between Hispanics and non-Hispanic Whites. For example, similar to education gaps between these two groups in general, impoverished Hispanics had lower average schooling levels than their non-Hispanic White counterparts (approximately 10 vs. 12 years of schooling in 2006–08). In addition, poor Hispanics were more likely than non-Hispanic Whites to be foreign-born, lack English-language fluency, and have more children and larger families. For example, only 53.1% of Hispanic men and 58.5% of Hispanic women living in poverty were proficient in English in 2006–08, compared to almost all non-Hispanics Whites.

While these differences may have contributed to the relatively high poverty rates of Hispanics, a comparison of labor market outcomes between poor Hispanics and non-Hispanic Whites reveals a different story. Impoverished Hispanics in 2006–08 earned more on average than their non-Hispanic White peers (56.2% more among men, and 27% more among women). They were also more likely to be employed, in the labor force, and have full-year/full-time jobs, than non-Hispanic Whites. For example, the employed represented 70% of impoverished Hispanic men (and the full-year/full-time represented 41.6%), compared to just 40.6% (and 17%) of impoverished non-Hispanic White men. Thus, poor Hispanics appear to have more favorable labor market outcomes compared to poor non-Hispanic Whites. Perhaps this disparity relates to the findings of Robin Anderson (2011), who reported that Hispanics had lower poverty exit rates, higher rates of chronic poverty, and higher poverty duration spells than non-Hispanic Whites. In addition, according to the United States Census Bureau, in 2010, 10.9% of Hispanics experienced deep poverty (when income falls below half of the poverty line) compared to 4.3% of non-Hispanic Whites.

In terms of gender-related differences in 2006–08, poor Hispanic women were almost twice as likely as their male counterparts to be single (74.9% vs. 37.1%), and they had lower rates of employment, labor force participation, and full-year/full-time employment (42.1%, 51.1%, and 17.6%, respectively, compared to 70.1%, 78.0%, and 41.6% for men). However, impoverished Hispanic women had slightly more education on average than impoverished Hispanic men, and greater English-language proficiency rates. The latter finding likely reflects the lower share of the foreign-born among women than men noted above.

Differences within the Hispanic population exist across various Hispanic subgroups with respect to human capital, family structures, and the presence of immigrants (for details, contact the author). For example, similar to the overall population, in 2006–08, the poor among the Hispanic subgroups had lower levels of schooling and English-language fluency, lower earnings, and lower employment and labor force participation rates than their non-impoverished peers. Moreover, Mexican Americans residing below the poverty line had larger families than Cubans, Puerto Ricans, and Dominicans, and they exhibited higher employment (including full-year/full-time) and labor force participation rates.

## DETERMINANTS OF POVERTY

To determine the extent to which socioeconomic and demographic factors discussed thus far significantly relate to the likelihood of being impoverished, a regression analysis is employed.[3] Table 4.2 shows the results from this exercise for Hispanic and non-Hispanic White men and women in 2006–08. Focusing on the first three characteristics in Table 4.2, which represent the labor market outcome measures, it is not surprising that greater employment (particularly full-year/full-time) and labor force participation

**TABLE 4.2   Determinants of Poverty for Hispanics and Non-Hispanic Whites: 2006–2008**

| Characteristic | Non-Hispanic White Men | Hispanic Men | Non-Hispanic White Women | Hispanic Women |
|---|---|---|---|---|
| Employed | −0.035** | −0.070*** | −0.063** | −0.130** |
|  | (0.001) | (0.005) | (0.002) | (0.007) |
| Labor Force Participant | −0.004** | −0.030** | −0.005** | −0.024** |
|  | (0.000) | (0.005) | (0.001) | (0.006) |
| Full-year, Full-time | −0.061** | −0.139** | −0.095** | −0.217** |
|  | (0.001) | (0.002) | (0.001) | (0.003) |
| Years of Schooling | −0.004** | −0.007** | −0.011** | −0.016** |
|  | (0.000) | (0.000) | (0.000) | (0.000) |
| English Proficiency | −0.019** | −0.069** | −0.030** | −0.099** |
|  | (0.002) | (0.002) | (0.004) | (0.004) |
| Children | 0.013** | 0.050** | 0.028** | 0.087** |
|  | (0.000) | (0.001) | (0.000) | (0.002) |
| Family Size | −0.006** | −0.020** | −0.020** | −0.044** |
|  | (0.000) | (0.001) | (0.000) | (0.001) |
| Age | −0.001** | −0.003** | −0.001** | −0.005** |
|  | (0.000) | (0.000) | (0.000) | (0.000) |
| Single | 0.033** | 0.039** | 0.074** | 0.216** |
|  | (0.001) | (0.002) | (0.001) | (0.003) |
| Foreign-born | 0.010** | 0.008** | 0.003* | −0.014** |
|  | (0.001) | (0.002) | (0.001) | (0.003) |
| Pseudo R-Squared | 0.291 | 0.192 | 0.339 | 0.303 |

*\*\*, \* Statistically significant at the one or five percent level.*
*Source:* Author's estimates using the 2006–2008 American Community Surveys.
*Notes:* Marginal effects are reported above which measure the effect of a one-unit increase in the independent variable on the probability that the dependent variable, poverty, equals one; see Note 3 for more details. The parentheses contain the standard errors of the marginal effects. The sample is restricted to household heads between the ages of 18–64. Controls for region were also included, but not shown above. The sample sizes are 1,007,224 non-Hispanic White men; 121,838 Hispanic men; 692,581 non-Hispanic White women; and 89,449 Hispanic women. These samples represent 92.9 million, 14.8 million, 66.0 million, and 10.6 million adult household heads

rates reduce poverty among all groups. Full-year/full-time employment appears to have the largest effect on poverty for Hispanic men and women, as this characteristic decreased the probability of being poor by 13.9 percentage points for Hispanic men and 21.7 percentage points for Hispanic women, other things the same. In addition, the labor market effects varied across groups: employment reduced the odds of being poor by 13 percentage points for Hispanic women in this time period, but only 6.3 percentage points for non-Hispanic White women and 3.5 percentage points for non-Hispanic men. Table 4.2 also shows that across all groups, full-year/full-time status mattered more for determining poverty among Hispanics than non-Hispanic Whites.

The findings for the human capital variables indicate that greater levels of schooling and English-language proficiency lowered the odds of being poor. For example, each year of schooling reduced these odds by 1.6 percentage points among Hispanic women, and 0.7 percentage points among Hispanic men. However it is important to note that the magnitudes of the marginal effects are lower for the human capital variables than for the labor market variables. Thus, the results suggest that the strongest *direct* determinants of poverty depend on poor employment outcomes (although these outcomes themselves depend on human capital, such that indirect effects are likely present).

Consistent with the literature, Table 4.2 reveals that children raise the probability of being poor, with this effect being largest for Hispanic women. While larger families can be associated with greater levels of poverty, the results suggest the opposite, as family size (beyond the number of children and marital status) related to a lower impoverishment likelihood in 2006–08.[4] Single household heads had a greater probability of being poor, with the largest effect observed for Hispanic women: single Hispanic women were 21.6 percentage points more likely than their otherwise similar married counterparts to reside below the poverty line in 2006–08, a significantly larger magnitude than for the other groups. Finally, other things the same, being foreign-born raised the likelihood of being poor for all groups during this time period, with the exception of Hispanic women. One possible explanation is that foreign-born Hispanic women had better employment opportunities than their U.S.-born counterparts due to a positive selection among immigrant women or a strong demand for their labor in the services industry.

While Table 4.2 shows that labor market and human capital variables are strong determinants of poverty, this table reveals that Hispanic women had the largest marginal effects across most of the variables included in the analysis. For example, full-year/full-time status lowered their probability of being poor by 21.7 percentage points in 2006–08. Thus, the findings suggest that policies to promote employment (particularly full-time), educational attainment, or programs to help single mothers have the potential to go far for impoverished Hispanic women.

The determinants of poverty were also estimated for various Hispanic subgroups (results available from the author). Similar to the findings presented in Table 4.2, employment, labor force participation, full-year, full-time status, schooling, and English-language proficiency reduced the odds of being impoverished across the subgroups. Again, the largest poverty-reducing effect in 2006–08 was full-year/full-time employment. Children and being single increased the likelihood of poverty, while family size (independent of the number of children and marital status) reduced it across all groups. Moreover, the foreign-born were more likely to be impoverished among Mexican Americans, Central Americans, South Americans, and Dominicans, but this was not the case for other Hispanic subgroups analyzed.

Comparing foreign-born with U.S.-born Hispanics, English-language proficiency, the number of children, and family size had the largest differences in the marginal probabilities of being impoverished in 2006–08 between the two groups. For example, English-language fluency reduced the odds of being poor by 9.8 percentage points among Hispanic immigrants, but 4.3 percentage points among Hispanic natives, other things the same.

Other interesting trends are observed across specific Hispanic origin groups. English-language proficiency had the largest effect for Dominicans, reducing their probability of impoverishment by 11.7 percentage points in 2006–08. The number of children also had a larger impact on the odds of residing in poverty for Dominicans than for other groups. Finally, being single had the largest effect for Mexican Americans, raising their likelihood of being poor by 13.2 percentage points, holding other characteristics constant. Thus, while the factors associated with poverty tend to be similar across groups, the magnitude of these effects appear to differ based on gender and detailed ethnicity. Differences in human capital and labor market opportunities, as well as the returns to human capital, exist across Hispanic subgroups.

## CONCLUSION

This chapter analyzes poverty rates and the factors associated with poverty between Hispanics and non-Hispanic Whites and among various Hispanic subgroups. The data show that aggregate poverty rates mask important differences across race, ethnicity, nativity, gender, and Hispanic-origin subgroups. For example, Mexican American men and Dominican women were more likely to be impoverished than other Hispanic groups of the same gender in 2006–08. In addition, Hispanic immigrants had higher poverty rates than other groups, even when controlling for other socioeconomic and demographic characteristics.

The analysis also shows that the factors associated with poverty vary across populations. Full-year/full-time employment is an important determinant in reducing poverty among Hispanic men and women. However, Hispanic women also experienced higher levels of poverty than men because of their low employment levels and large share of single-headed households. In sum, the data reveal that the poor are not a homogeneous group. Efforts to reduce poverty among Hispanics (and other populations) must not only address ways to improve their educational attainment and labor market outcomes, but should also include policies that aim to improve the English-language proficiency and child-care for single mothers.

## NOTES

1. The U.S. Census Bureau defines a primary family as a group of persons related to the head of the household and a primary individual as a household head residing without relatives.

2. The Census Bureau calculates poverty as each family's total income as a percentage of the poverty thresholds established by the Social Security Administration; as such, the same value is assigned to all members of each family. These thresholds were developed in 1963–64 by Mollie Orshansky, an economist who worked for the Social Security Administration. Survey data on food consumption from the Department of Agriculture showed that, in 1955, families of three or more typically spent one-third of their income on food. The U.S. Department of Agriculture also established several nutritionally adequate food plans. The least costly food plan was the economy food plan. Thus, the poverty level was set at three times the cost of the economy food plan. The thresholds are revised annually using the Consumer Price Index (CPI) to reflect changes in the cost of living. One criticism is that these thresholds remain the same for all parts of the country and are not adjusted for differences in the cost of living across regional, state, or local levels (e.g., Fisher, 1992). Another criticism is that the level of income used to calculate the poverty rate does not include in-kind transfers, child care subsidies, and the Earned Income Tax Credit, all of which increase the economic well-being of the family, nor does it include work expenses or taxes paid, which lower a family's economic well-being (Meyer & Wallace 2009; Fisher, 1992).

3. A probit model is employed to analyze which socioeconomic and demographic factors significantly relate to the probability of being in poverty. This model is used because of the dichotomous nature of the dependent variable, which equals one for impoverished household heads and equals zero otherwise. Estimating the probit equation allows us to determine which factors have a significant effect on the probability of being impoverished and how these effects vary across groups. The results from this probit analysis (shown in

Table 4.2) indicate that many of the characteristics significantly relate to the odds of residing in poverty at the one-percent level. A more comprehensible way to interpret the probit results is to compute the marginal probabilities, which measure the effect of a one-unit increase in the independent variable on the probability that someone is poor. These marginal probabilities are evaluated at the mean for continuous independent variables, and going from zero to one for binary variables. Contact the author for more specific details.

4.  When the probit equation is estimated without controlling for single status and number of children, the marginal effects on family size remain negative with an exception for Hispanic men, where the marginal effect becomes positive.

## REFERENCES

Anderson, R. (2011). Dynamics of economic well-being: Poverty, 2004–2006. *Current population reports* (pp. 70–123). Washington: U.S. Government Printing Office, U.S. Census Bureau.

Bartik, T. (2001). *Jobs for the poor: Can labor demand policies help?* New York: Russell Sage Foundation.

Blank, R. M. (2000). Fighting poverty: Lessons from recent U.S. history. *Journal of Economic Perspectives, 14*(2), 3–19.

Blank, R. M. (2003). Selecting among anti-poverty policies: Can an economist be both critical and caring? *Review of Social Economy, 4*, 447–469.

Blank, R. M. (2009). Economic change and the structure of opportunity for less-skilled workers. In M. Cancian & S. Danziger (Eds.), *Changing poverty changing policies* (pp. 63–91). New York: Russell Sage Foundation.

Borjas, G. (2006). Wage trends among disadvantaged minorities. In R. M. Blank, S. H. Danziger & R. F. Schoeni (Eds.), *Working and poor: How economic and policy changes are affecting low-wage workers* (pp. 59–86). New York: Russell Sage Foundation.

Cancian, M., & Danziger, S. (2009). Changing poverty and changing antipoverty policies. In M. Cancian & S. Danziger (Eds.), *Changing poverty changing policies* (pp. 1–31). New York: Russell Sage Foundation.

Durlauf, S. N. (2001). The memberships theory of poverty: The role of group affiliations in determining socioeconomic outcomes. In S. H. Danziger & R. H. Haveman (Eds.), *Understanding poverty* (pp. 359–391). New York: Russell Sage Foundation.

Fisher, G. (1992). The development and history of the poverty thresholds. *Social Security Bulletin, 55*(4), 3–14.

Freeman, R. (2001). The rising tide lifts...? In S. H. Danziger & R. H. Haveman (Eds.), *Understanding poverty* (pp. 97–192). New York: Russell Sage Foundation.

Hoynes, H. W., Page, M. E., & Stevens, A. H. (2006). Poverty in America: Trends and explanations. *Journal of Economic Perspectives, 20*(1), 47–68.

Iceland, J. (2003). Why poverty remains high: The role of income growth, economic inequality, and changes in family structure, 1949–1999. *Demography, 40*(3), 499–519.

Kochhar, R. (2008). Latino labor report, 2008: Construction reverses job growth for Latinos. *Pew Hispanic Research Center Report.* Washington, DC: Pew Hispanic Center.

Meyer, D. R., & Wallace, G. L. (2009). Poverty levels and trends in comparative perspective. In M. Cancian & S. Danziger (Eds.), *Changing poverty changing policies* (pp. 35–62). New York: Russell Sage Foundation.

Pager, D. (2003). The mark of a criminal record. *American Journal of Sociology, 108,* 937–75.

Pew Hispanic Center. (2008). *Statistical portrait of Hispanics in the United States, 2008,* Washington, D.C.: Pew Hispanic Center.

Pew Hispanic Center. (2011). Country of origin profiles found at http://www.pewhispanic.org/2011/05/26/country-of-origin-profiles/

Raphael, S. (2007). Early incarceration spells and the transition to adulthood. In S. Danziger & C. Rouse (Eds.), *The price of independence.* New York: Russell Sage Foundation.

Raphael, S., & Smolensky, E. (2009). Immigration and poverty in the United States. In M. Cancian & S. Danziger (Eds), *Changing poverty changing policies* (pp. 122–150). New York: Russell Sage Foundation.

Ruggles, S. J., Alexander, T., Genadek, K., Goeken, R., Schroeder, M.B., & Sobek, M. (2010). *Integrated public use microdata series: Version 5.0* [Machine-readable database]. Minneapolis: University of Minnesota, www.ipums.org.

Simms, M. (2009). *Tailoring assistance: How policy can address diverse deeds within the poverty population.* Urban Institute.

Steffensmeier, D., & Demuth, S. (2001). Ethnicity and judges' sentencing decisions: Hispanic-Black–White comparisons. *Criminology, 39,* 145–178.

Sullivan, D. H., & Ziegert, A. L. (2008). Hispanic immigrant poverty: Does ethnic origin matter? *Population Research Policy Review, 27,* 667–687.

U.S. Bureau of the Census. (2008). *Income, poverty, and health insurance coverage in the United States: 2008,* Report P60, n. 236, Table 4, pp. 14.

Wheelock, D., & Uggen, C. (2008). Punishment, crime, and poverty. In A. C. Lin & D. R. Harris (Eds.), *The colors of poverty: Why racial and ethnic disparities persist* (pp. 261–92). New York: Russell Sage Foundation.

Yinger, J. (2001). Housing discrimination and residential segregation as causes of poverty. In S. H. Danziger & R. H. Haveman (Eds), *Understanding poverty* (pp. 359–391). New York: Russell Sage Foundation.

CHAPTER 5

# A MULTILEVEL ANALYSIS OF LATINOS' ECONOMIC INEQUALITY

## A Test of the Minority Group Threat Theory

**Carlos Siordia**
*University of Texas Medical Branch*

**Ruben Antonio Farias**
*Texas A&M University*

In September 2010 the news media alerted the public that: the "ranks of the working-age poor climbed to the highest level since the 1960s . . . leaving one in seven Americans in poverty" (CBS News, 2010). Four months later, in January 2011, the media raised the alarm further by reporting that the "number of poor people in the United States is millions higher than previously known, with one in six Americans" struggling in poverty (CBS News, 2011). Finally, the *New York Times* ran a story on the United States' "lost de-

*The Economic Status of the Hispanic Population,* pages 65–79
Copyright © 2013 by Information Age Publishing
All rights of reproduction in any form reserved.

cade," showing that the recent increase in the depth and severity of poverty underscored the overall economic challenges facing a substantial portion of Americans. As the author reports, "[national poverty data] brought into sharp relief the toll the past decade—including the painful declines of the financial crisis and recession—had taken on Americans at the middle and lower parts of the income ladder (Tavernise, 2011). Overall, the mass media's message is clear: *many U.S. residents are experiencing financial troubles.*

Which individuals and groups have been adversely affected by the economic downturn of the last decade? A closer look at poverty data reveals that: *financial trouble has affected some racial/ethnic groups more severely than others.* Notably, Latinos and Blacks have been the two most distressed racial groups with 26% of Latinos and 27% of African Americans living in poverty (Tavernise, 2011). In contrast, the poverty rate among non-Hispanic Whites stands at 9.9%. Due to the volume's focus on Latinos,[1] this chapter concentrates on Latino poverty in the United States, extending the discussion from the previous chapter.

Studying Latino poverty—especially in relation to non-Hispanic Whites—is important. Such information contributes to the ongoing national discussions (as exemplified in the media, politics, and academic circles) on how, if at all, the increase in the Latino population will "change the face" of the United States. Some commentators argue that Latinos' growing group size (and hence influence) will weaken and disunite the nation-state (for an interesting discussion see the 2004 study by R. Yzaguirre and his colleagues). Leo Chavez (2008) has called such rhetoric the "Latino Threat Narrative," which is a pervasive national narrative that portrays Latinos in general, and people of Mexican origin in particular, as a "danger" to the basic sovereignty of the United States nation-state. In contrast, many observers conjecture that in the near future (around the time when Latinos are projected to become largest racial-ethnic group in the United States) the nation will become a more multicultural and racially egalitarian nation.

## POVERTY IN THE UNITED STATES

Notwithstanding numerous governmental and private initiatives, poverty levels in the United States were roughly the same in 1980 as in 2009. As reported by the Annual Social and Economic Supplement (ASEC) from the Current Population Survey, in 1980, about 13% of the U.S. population lived at or below the poverty line, compared to 14% in 2009. The one percentage-point difference between these two times hides the fact that in 2009 there was a bigger population base—which means there are more people living in poverty now than thirty years ago.

Recent U.S. Census Bureau reports indicate that poverty has, in fact, increased in the last couple of years. For instance, there was a statistically significant increase in the poverty rate from 2008 (13.2%) to 2009 (14.3%) (DeNavas-Walt, Bernadette, & Smith, 2010). In absolute numbers, the number of people living in poverty increased from 39.8 million in 2008 to 43.6 million in 2009. The 2009 poverty rate was the highest since 1994, but lower than the first official poverty rate estimate (of 22.4%) in 1959.

What are some notable characteristics of contemporary poverty? The recent increase in poverty is characterized by geographic and demographic concentration. In terms of geography, previous publications indicate that 13 states contain almost two thirds of the individuals living in poverty (see Bishaw & Macartney, 2010, Figure 1). Poverty is not only geographically clustered along southern states (Holt, 2007); it is also concentrated along detectable racial/ethnic groups. For example, of the 43 million people living in poverty during the 2009 survey period, non-Hispanic Whites only had 9.4% (or about 1 in every 10) of their population living in poverty while more than one in every four Latinos (or 25.3%) were in poverty (DeNavas-Walt, Bernadette, & Smith, 2010). In sum, two trends are clear from the poverty data:

1. Economic recessions and booms have come and gone while poverty has persistently retained its firm place in American society.
2. The absolute number of people categorized as poor in 2009 is the largest since poverty estimates were first published.

The history of poverty in the United States is admittedly complex. Nevertheless, people continue to enter, exit, and remain in poverty during their lifetime. The very real consequences of poverty are important points to remember. As we next discuss, the minority group threat theory highlights such consequences on the lives of racial-ethnic minorities.

## GROUP THREAT THEORY

Forty years ago, it was eloquently stated that when "a person thinks, more than one generation's passions and images think in him" (Novak, 1972, p. 32). In this section we investigate *how* the percent of Latinos in an area of residence is associated with the likelihood of experiencing poverty. Prior research demonstrates that there are significant statistical associations between poverty, racial-ethnic status, and place level measures (e.g., Siordia, 2011). Before exploring these associations, a review of the chapter's main theory is in order. In particular, the review underscores how the percent of Latinos in the area of residence influences an individual's chances for experiencing poverty—*over and above the influence of the individual characteristics.* In short, the occurrence of poverty is significantly influenced by geographic and place-level attributes.

Huber M. Blalock Jr. (1970) formulated empirically testable propositions on minority-group relations.[2] He outlined a theory with two primary components:

1. Groups of individuals who are aligned by some detectable characteristic (e.g., race-ethnicity) seek out ways to either obtain or retain a "dominant group" status.
2. When the dominant group (i.e., the one with the largest control over political, economic, and social power) perceives that a competing group is acquiring power, they fear them and seek ways to hinder or prohibit the subordinate group from advancing.[3]

In other words, when inter-group competition for tangible (e.g., money) and intangible (e.g., language) resources increases, perceptions of out-groups as threats increase within the dominant group. Dominant group members then respond with "exclusionary anti-outgroup attitudes" which serve to protect their individual and group interests (Schlueter & Scheepers, 2010).

The most pertinent component of Blalock's minority group threat theory is that "exposure to large numbers of minority members" threatens "*individual* members of the dominant group" (Blalock, 1970, p. 28 italics by original author). Rephrased to fit our case, when non-Hispanic White group members perceive a growth in the Latino population and interpret it as a threat, non-Hispanic White *individual* members will act in such a way so as to reduce their level of fear.

Under what specific conditions will the dominant group act, via discrimination, to maintain group control? A discriminatory response occurs when non-Hispanic Whites:

1. Perceive an increase in the Latino population
2. Interpret the increase as posing a threat.

In the words of Gary Becker (1971, p. 123), "tastes for discrimination against non-whites vary directly with their proportion in a community." Blalock's theory directly links a minority group's population size with perceived fear in the dominant group. The higher the population size of a minority group, the more the group can be seen as posing a threat to the dominant one.

It is important to consider how "threats combine with personality variables to produce motivation to discriminate" (Blalock, 1970, p. 28), because "different kinds of persons will not be similarly motivated by the minority percentage variable" (Blalock, 1970, p. 31). The main component of the group threat theory—that an increase in a minority group's population leads to perceived fear and discriminatory actions—underscores another important proposition of the theory: the main motivation compelling dominant group discrimination is the desire to keep group control. Ultimately, in response to the perceived threat (fear) of the minority group, the dominant group works to maintain their privileged status.

How does Blalock's theory apply to the case of Latinos? We expect that as the percent of Latinos in an area of residence increases, fears of them by non-Hispanic Whites will increase, such that they would respond to increase their ability to retain political and economic control. Specifically, the rise in fear among non-Hispanic Whites can result in discriminatory practices against Latinos—which can lead to economic marginalization. By arguing that Latino poverty is in part a product of discrimination,[4] we contribute to the literature describing the process by which oppressed groups become the recipients of their disadvantages.

What is the result of long term discrimination of the dominant group (non-Hispanic Whites) against the minority group (Latinos)? When discriminatory behaviors by non-Hispanic White individuals are sustained over time, they form structural elements (e.g., laws, financial agencies, school funding policies) that systematically inhibit Latinos from obtaining social and human capital resources. According to Herbert Blumer (1958), when historically advantaged group members (in our case non-Hispanic Whites) perceive minority-group members (in our case Latinos) as threatening their entitlements, non-Hispanic Whites manifest their prejudice towards the challenging minority group. The positive association between discrimination and minority presence occurs because similarly motivated non-Hispanic Whites "interact with each other in such a way as to bring about concerted action leading to actual discrimination" (Blalock, 1970, p. 28). This is how individual-level behaviors combine over time to create durable and unjust discriminatory distributive processes (Massey, 2007). If non-Hispanic White group members discriminate similarly and consistently against Latinos, then their behaviors will contribute towards instituting systemic discriminatory practices that collectively constrain Latinos.

Some have convincingly argued that Latinos are seen by some as a threat to the "American way of life" (Sáenz, Cready, & Morales, 2007). When thinking of how individual-level behaviors combine to form macro-level social structures, we can frame our discussion on racial-ethnic discrimination as follows. The more non-Hispanic Whites are threatened by Latinos, the more they cooperate, and the more likely discrimination against Latino occurs. Consequently, as the Latino population proliferation continues, it could represent a threat that fuels the prevailing stratification system by allowing non-Hispanic Whites the ability to erect "formidable structural obstacles" (Sáenz, 1997, p. 207)

Prior research has given support to Blalock's relative group size-inequality theory in the case of Latinos. For example, Rogelio Sáenz (1997) found a positive relationship between the relative size of the Chicano population and the group's poverty rate. Additionally, related work has shown that Latinos residing in communities with heavy co-ethnic concentrations have a labor market penalty (e.g., Bean & Tienda, 1987; Cort, 2011; Kaplan & Douzet, 2011; Wang, 2010). Recent arguments have advanced "that the animosity toward Latinos by both the majority white *and* minority Black populations may be more intense than those shaping contemporary White-Black relations" (Markert, 2010). Support for Blalock's power-threat theory has been given elsewhere (Kane, 2003), and some have pointed out that in highly segregated areas "the relative size of the Latino population is a predictor of fear of crime among White residents" (Eitle & Taylor, 2008, p. 1102).

A great amount of space is dedicated elsewhere (Siordia, 2011) towards delineating the assumptions of how "individual goals, motives, and needs are major causal agents in social systems" (Blalock, 1970, p. 28). For now, there is one theoretical premise (as adapted from Blalock) that will suffice in advancing our understanding of the ethno-racial discrimination-poverty link. We outline and adapt it to our Latino versus non-Hispanic White comparison. As may be clear by now, we perceive non-Hispanic Whites to be the dominant racial-ethnic group in the United States. We make this the case because non-Hispanic Whites have historically controlled most of the governmental, economic, and social structures in the United States; they "have more balanced distribution of labor and capital" (Becker, 1971, p. 32) than Latinos. Thus, when we mention the dominant group in the context of our chapter, we are referring to non-Hispanic Whites.

In passing, we would like the reader to be aware of an extensive literature on how inter-group contact works (see Allport, 1954). It is beyond the scope of this chapter to address how this topic plays a role in our investigation. In the most general sense we should keep in mind that "since people discriminate little against those with whom they have only indirect [contact] in the market place, some direct contact must be necessary for the development of a desire to discriminate" (Becker, 1971, p. 154). On the one hand, inter-ethnic contact can result in the reduction of racial-ethnic discrimination under the right circumstances (Burton-Chelley, Ross-Gillespie, & West, 2010). On the other hand, the increased presence of Latinos may escalate the potential for non-Hispanic Whites to be in contact with them, which may in turn provide the social-psychological material necessary for fearing Latinos and subsequently desiring to discriminate against them. We bring up the "contact hypothesis" to simply point out that our chapter only focuses on the "negative aspects" arriving from inter-ethnic contact.

By following our delineated theoretical views, we utilize an empirical model to measure how Latinos' co-ethnic concentration relates their likelihood of being in poverty when compared to non-Hispanic Whites. Our quantitative investigation focuses on individuals as units of analysis while using macro-level variables as indicators of racial-ethnic exposure to Latinos. In particular, our analysis estimates how the percentage of Latinos in the area of residence affects a Latino's likelihood of being in poverty after accounting for several other individual-level and context-level factors. The latter factors (also referred to as macro-level factors) pertain to the characteristics of the geographic area in which the individual resides.

The investigation in effect tests how "contextual effects" (Blalock, 1970, p. 26) affect the Latino status with respect to the likelihood of being in poverty. Even though our model allows for comparisons between non-Hispanic-Blacks to non-Hispanic Whites, such a discussion deserves detailed attention, which is not possible in this chapter.

## DATA AND METHODOLOGY

Our analysis of Latino poverty is conducted using a Public Use Microdata Sample (PUMS) from the American Community Survey (ACS), specifically the ACS 2005–2007 three-year PUMS files. The Data Appendix chapter provides more information on the ACS. For the United States government to release microdata files, they must employ various techniques to ensure the confidentiality of survey participants, including limiting the ability of public users to geographically locate respondents. The U.S. Census Bureau protects the identity of survey participants by introducing small demographic alterations to the sample and by only allowing public data users the ability to physically locate respondents to geographical areas with at least 100,000 people, called Public Use Microdata Areas (PUMAs). PUMAs are the smallest identifiable geographic unit. As such, our measure of Latino concentration is the percentage of Latinos in the PUMA.

Our sample of interest only includes individuals ages 20–64 who directly participated in the survey, and who resided in one of the mainland contiguous states (and D.C.).[5] Our primary individual-level variable of interest is an individual's racial-ethnic identity. We use ethnicity along with race because previous research has found that "people with specific ethnic self-conceptions" use different self-images in the course of interaction with others (Sáenz & Aguirre, 1991, p. 17). Given this chapter's focus, the sample only includes Latinos/as, single-race non-Hispanic-Blacks, and single-race non-Hispanic-Whites (referred to here as non-Hispanic Whites).

It is important to note that "ethnicity" is an inherently qualitative and complicated concept first instrumentalized at a large scale by the United States government to capture a broad group of peoples. The U.S. Census Bureau collects race and Hispanic-origin information following the guidance of the United States Office of Management and Budget—which defines "Hispanic" as a person of Cuban, Mexican, Puerto Rican, South or Central American, or other Spanish culture or origin regardless of race. As a consequence of this grouping scheme, and since the umbrella term includes a very identity-fluid group of individuals, Hispanics/Latinos are a heterogeneous ethnic group.

We now describe our empirical model for our analysis. Our empirical model predicts the likelihood of being in poverty when controlling for observable individual-level and geographic-level characteristics.[6] Since our interpretation focuses on contrasting how Latinos differ in their odds of being in poverty with non-Hispanic Whites, the latter group represents the reference category. Studies, including the previous chapter, have shown that racial-ethnic minorities are more likely than non-Hispanic Whites to be in poverty—this is not our primary interest (although the models confirm it). The primary question under investigation is on how the Latino concentration at the PUMA-level influences the Latino status as it predicts the likelihood of being in poverty.

A driving motivation behind this investigation is that many poverty-related studies have been lacking in one respect: the recognition and modeling of multilevel data. If racial-ethnic context matters, then accounting for it is not only important but *necessary*. More generally, our basic argument "...is that through its opportunity structure, the place of residence affects the ability of households to raise their economic status and avoid falling into poverty, above and beyond the human resources and work behavior of its residents" (Lewin, Stier, & Caspi-Dror, 2006, p. 178). In short, place matters.

## SAMPLE CHARACTERISTICS AND EMPIRICAL FINDINGS

As seen in Table 5.1, the average age of individuals in our analytic sample was 45, about 57% of them were male, 14% had some form of disability, 58% were married, about 15% had served in the military at some point in their lifetime, and approximately 90% had a high school degree and beyond. From this table, Latinos (of all races) made up 11% of the sample, and that non-Hispanic Whites comprise the majority (79%). Nearly four out of five individuals in our sample were U.S.-born, while immigrants were, on average, 21 years of age at time of arrival.

**TABLE 5.1   Characteristics of Latinos, Non-Hispanic Blacks, and Non-Hispanic Whites: 2005–2007**

| Characteristic | All | Latinos | Non-Hispanic Blacks | Non-Hispanic Whites |
|---|---|---|---|---|
| **Panel A: Individual-level characteristics** | | | | |
| In poverty | 10% | 17% | 20% | 7% |
| Latinos | 11% | 100% | — | — |
| Non-Hispanic Blacks | 10% | — | 100% | — |
| Non-Hispanic Whites | 79% | — | — | 100% |
| U.S.-born | 90% | 46% | 90% | 96% |
| Age at immigration (range: 20-64 years) | 21 | 22 | 24 | 20 |
| Bilingual | 10% | 55% | 6% | 4% |
| Monolingual non-English household | 3% | 25% | 1% | 0.4% |
| Age (range: 20-64 years) | 45 | 41 | 44 | 46 |
| Male | 57% | 58% | 40% | 60% |
| Disabled | 14% | 13% | 20% | 14% |
| Married | 58% | 59% | 36% | 61% |
| Served in Military | 15% | 7% | 13% | 16% |
| At least a high school education | 90% | 68% | 85% | 93% |
| **Panel B: Area-level variables** | | | | |
| Percent Latinos | 14% | — | — | — |
| Percent Non-Hispanic Blacks | 13% | — | — | — |
| Percent with a bachelors degree and beyond | 19% | — | — | — |

*Source:* Authors' estimates using 2005-2007 ACS data in the IPUMS. The sample only contains the reference persons ages 20–64 who filled out the questionnaire; see the text for more information.

About one in every ten persons in our sample resided below the poverty line in 2005–07. In terms of the association of poverty with race and ethnicity, 17% of Latinos, and 20% of non-Hispanic Blacks were impoverished, compared to only 7% of non-Hispanic Whites. When it comes to language, 10% were bilingual (speak another language other than English at home and speak English "very well" or "well") and 3% were monolingual in a non-English language (i.e., they speak English "not well" or "not at all"). Unfortunately, the bilingual variable offers little insight on the details of bilingualism; since it measures language spoken at home, it fails to capture those who may be bilingual but lived in a monolingual English household. Consequently, as the bilingual variable is constructed here, it only informs us that the individual spoke English and another language at home.

From the geographic-level characteristics in Table 5.1, PUMAs in 2005–07 averaged a 14-percent Latino population concentration, followed by an average 13% non-Hispanic Black population concentration. When it comes to formal educational attainment, on average, the PUMAs had populations in which 19% have a bachelor's degree and beyond.

We now turn to the findings from our empirical model, which predicts a persons' likelihood of being in poverty when controlling for other characteristics. Table 5.2 only consists of "percent change" values, which are the odds ratio minus one times 100. The "direct effect" column reflects the micro-level association between the variable and the outcome (i.e., likelihood of being in poverty). The "Area's % Latino" column shows the cross-level interaction between the area's Latino concentration

**TABLE 5.2  Individual-Level and Geographic-Level Determinants of the Likelihood of Residing below the Poverty Line: 2005–2007**

| Characteristic | Direct Effect (I) | Area's % Latino (II) | Area's % Non-Hispanic-Black (III) | Area's % College Graduates (IV) |
|---|---|---|---|---|
| Intercept | 46%* | −66%* | −48%* | −97%* |
| **Racial-ethnic group** | | | | |
| Latino | 26%* | 20%* | 72%* | −15% |
| Non-Hispanic Black | 74%* | 9% | 15% | 42%* |
| **Demographic covariates** | | | | |
| U.S.-born | −25%* | −17%* | 33%* | 15% |
| Age at immigration | 1%* | −1%* | −2%* | 1% |
| Bilingual | 20%* | −17%* | −15%* | 13% |
| Non-English monolingual household | 26%* | 26%* | −13% | 363% |
| Age | −4%* | 1%* | 0.20% | −1% |
| Male | −55%* | 28%* | 15%* | 195%* |
| Disabled | 279%* | −41%* | −20%* | 91%* |
| Married | −74%* | 146%* | 67%* | −49%* |
| Served | −11%* | −17%* | −16%* | 47%* |
| At least a high school education | −65%* | 49%* | −2% | −21%* |

* Statistically significant at conventional levels.

*Source:* Authors' estimates using 2005–2007 ACS data in the IPUMS for the reference persons ages 20–64.

*Notes:* Column I shows the percent change in odds ratio for the individual-level relationship between the characteristics and the probability of being impoverished. The remaining columns show the percent changes in the odds ratio for the cross-level interactions with the (1) percentage of Latinos in the PUMA (Column II), percentage of non-Hispanic Blacks in the PUMA (Column III), and (3) the percentage of individuals with a bachelors degree or higher in the PUMA (Column IV).

and the variable in the row. Readers may contact the authors for a more detailed set of results.

We focus on the findings for the two primary coefficients of interest: how being Latino influences the chances of being in poverty, other things the same, as well as how the geographic Latino concentration relates to these chances. At the individual-level, our results indicate that in 2005–07, Latinos had a 25% *greater* likelihood of being in poverty than otherwise similar non-Hispanic-Whites. This confirms other reports that Latinos are more likely to experience poverty than non-Hispanic Whites. Our results indicate that when it comes to predicting the likelihood of poverty, being a Latino is a disadvantage, even when controlling for other observable characteristics (such as age, English-language fluency, etc.) related to the odds of being in poverty.

It is worth mentioning that all the other individual-level characteristics played a role in the likelihood of being poor. Being female, disabled, having less than a high school education, and not residing in a monolingual-English household, for example, all increased this likelihood. Since these conditions are prevalent among Latinos, they compound the risk of impoverishment within this population.

Just as Blalock's group threat hypothesis predicted, moreover, Table 5.2 suggests that as the concentration of Latinos increases, a Latino's chances of being in poverty increase further as well—a social context influence that is above and beyond their individual-level characteristics. When investigating the *indirect effects* of the share of Latinos on the association between Latinos and the odds of being in poverty, we find that the "Latino disadvantage" increases with the concentration of Latinos in the PUMA of residence. Although not shown here, the raw estimated coefficient for this cross-level interaction is 0.22, which in technical terms means that for every increase of 0.01 in a community's percent Latino, the micro-level association between "Latino and poverty" status on the log odds of being in poverty increase by 0.0022%.[7]

In short, our hypothesis is supported because we find that as the geographic presence of Latinos increases, the odds of being in poverty rise for Latinos. Our investigation is important because Blalock's proposition—a minority-group's proliferation increases discrimination against them—is supported in our findings in the context of Latinos.

The fundamental argument underlying this investigation suggests that economic inequality occurs on an unequal basis, as a function of ascribed and attained characteristics in a socially stratified society. We do not appear to be born into a level-playing field. The existence of poverty has material consequences with the potential to alter our society, for better or worse. Since Latinos are, and will continue to be, a force in the formation of North America, their observed disadvantage can affect all U.S. residents. If fear continues to rise and produce discriminatory behaviors that victimize the economic condition of Latinos, then Latinos might eventually learn to abstain from participating in the U.S. democracy experiment.

## CONCLUSION

The chapter began by arguing and providing evidence for how social disequilibrium asymmetrically affects Latinos. Seeking the cause of economic inequality is primarily driven by the desire to blame somebody. Because the subtle but prevalent belief is that if the source of a problem is found, a solution is possible. Finding the source(s) of Latino inequality is the first step towards developing a response that may negate the initial formation of inequality—because Latino poverty is a national issue, not just a Latino issue.

Both "structure" and "agency" factors affect a Latino's life chances. Our chapter offers evidence for how structural factors affect Latinos. As with all academic investigations, there are some limitations with the present study. For example, the measure of poverty is bounded in how the U.S. federal government measures it. Also, we frame poverty as the product of discrimination and thus interpret its presence as evidence that discriminatory practices have negatively affected Latinos. Beyond these measurement assumptions and limitations, and because we are using cross-sectional data, we are unable to determine how "lifetime factors" (e.g., childhood economic status) play a role in a Latino's adult poverty status. On a more theoretical aspect, our study is limited in that it assumes individual-level prejudices by non-Hispanic Whites coalesce to influence the formation of unjust and systematic discriminatory systems against Latinos, without regard to how agency plays a role.[8]

Notwithstanding these limitations, our investigation is valuable because it lends support to the minority-group threat theory by showing that a Latino's co-ethnic concentration influences his/her chances of being in poverty. Future research should investigate the theoretical essence driving multilevel modeling. First, researchers should seek to better measure how people feel they belong to a community. Then, they should determine if the geographical boundaries of said community can be drawn in such a way so as to apply to most people's perception of a "neighborhood." We suspect standardizing community geographical boundarization will prove challenging since people may vary greatly in their perceptions of where their community starts and ends. Lastly, more standardized measures on the social characteristics of environment should be created. These efforts will allow for a more scientific measure of how minority population growth is perceived by non-Hispanic Whites.

Blalock's predictions have not been falsified here. If Blalock's theories are correct and Latino's proliferation in the United States continues, then fear, conflict, and discrimination may continue to rise. One of the major contributions of this chapter lies in the empirical modeling of minority-group status related variables in the prediction of poverty. We are unable to falsify the main argument that Latinos are at a disadvantage when compared to non-Hispanic Whites, and that their co-ethnic concentration further aggravates their individual-level economic-penalty.

## NOTES

1. Please note that because the "Hispanic" label is a contested category within some academic circles, we opted to use Latino (Aguirre & Turner, 2011). In truth, some investigations have found that Latinos/as prefer to ethnically identify with a "national origin" label and that such preference can even vary by geographical settings (e.g., Kiang, Perreira, & Fuligni, 2011). We use the term Latino since in our models we include all sub-ethnic groups subsume under the ethnic label (e.g., Mexicans, Dominicans, Puerto Ricans, etc.). It is more appropriate to use Latinos/as, but we have chosen to use masculine-singular "Latino(s)" in order to keep chapter more readable. We use the term racial-ethnic status in reference to "racial and ethnic" groupings outlined in greater detail in the methods section of the chapter.

2. We reference Blalock's 1970 paper because it more clearly delineates all his previous and subsequent work. It should be noted that the "group threat" idea was first introduced to academic literature more than 60 years ago by a Texan (Key, 1949) and was subsequently brought into the academic main stage by Blalock and others.

3. A full discussion, explaining the five general ways in which fear towards minorities occurs is given elsewhere, as are the details underlying the theoretical assumptions in this area of research (Siordia, 2011).

4. It is important to note here that socioeconomic inequality is a resultant of discriminatory behavior *and* "of other factors as well" (Blalock, 1970, p. 17). A full discussion on the "other factors" is important but beyond the scope of this study. We do however acknowledge that there are components (e.g., agency, biology, etc.) beyond social structures that can influence life chances. Some of these other factors were discussed in the previous chapter.

5. More technically, we only include "reference" persons in ACS data (i.e., those who filled out the questionnaire) because *self-identification* on both the race and ethnic variable matters deeply. Age selection is done to increase our chances of only evaluating working-age adults. Also, we only selected states in the mainland because we are unsure if spatial autocorrelation may be playing a role in the diffusion of Latino population.

6. The federal government determines "poverty thresholds" by family types to determine if individuals are in poverty (for more details see http://aspe.hhs.gov/poverty/11poverty.shtml). Their poverty thresholds do not vary geo-

graphically, and as such, do not account for the relative cost of living. The thresholds are however annually updated for inflation using the Consumer Price Index.

7. The reason why the value is moved two decimal places to the rights is that the *percent Latino* variable is measured as a proportion that ranges from 0.00 to 0.98. This means that a one unit change in the *percent Latino* variable would result in a change in the log-odds of 0.21. But a change of 0.01 in the same variable results in a change in the log-odds of 0.0021.

8. Hobbes (1839) first introduced the term "agency" to social science over 170 years ago. However, the agency versus structure debate remains unresolved (e.g., see Fuchs, 2001, p. 24). "Systemic discrimination" involves a pattern where differential treatment has deep and broad impacts on people (e.g., see Feagin, 2006).

# REFERENCES

Aguirre, A., & Turner, J. H. (2011). *American ethnicity: The dynamics and consequences of discrimination.* New York: McGraw-Hill.

Allport, G. W. (1954). *The nature of prejudice.* Garden City, NY: Doubleday.

Becker, G. S. (1971). *Human capital: A theoretical and empirical analysis, with special reference to education.* Chicago: University of Chicago Press.

Bean, F. D., & Tienda, M. (1987). *The Hispanic population of the United States.* New York: Russell Sage Foundation.

Bishaw, A., & Macartney. S. (2010). U.S. Census Bureau, American Community Survey Briefs, ACSBR/09-1, *Poverty: 2008 and 2009,* U.S. Government Printing Office, Washington, DC.

Blalock, Jr., H. M. (1970). *Toward a theory of minority-group relations.* New York: Capricorn Books.

Blumer, H. (1958). Race prejudice as a sense of group position. *Pacific Sociological Review, 1,* 3–7.

Burton-Chellew, M. N., Ross-Gillespie, A, & West, S. A. (2010). Cooperation in humans: Competition between groups and proximate emotions. *Evolution and Human Behavior, 31,* 104–108.

Cort, D. A. (2011). Reexamining the ethnic hierarchy of locational attainment: Evidence from Los Angeles. *Social Science Research, 40*(6), 1521–1533.

Chavez, L. R. (2008). *The Latino threat: Constructing immigrants, citizens, and the nation.* Palo Alto: Stanford University Press.

DeNavas-Walt, C., Bernadette D. P., & Smith, J. C. (2010). U.S. Census Bureau, Current Population Reports, P60–238, *Income, poverty, and health insurance coverage in the United States: 2009,* U.S. Government Printing Office, Washington, D.C.

Eitle, D., & Taylor, J. (2008). Are Hispanics the new "threat"? Minority group threat and fear of crime in Miami-Dade county. *Social Science Research, 37,* 1102–1115.

Feagin, J. R. (2006). *Systemic racism: A theory of oppression.* New York, NY: Routledge

Holt, J. B. (2007). The topography of poverty in the United States: A spatial analysis using county-level data from the community health status indicators project. *Preventing Chronic Disease, 4,* 4–9.

Kane, R. J. (2003). Social control in the metropolis: A community-level examination of the minority group-threat hypothesis. *Justice Quarterly, 20*, 265–95.

Kaplan, D. H., & Douzet, F. (2011). Research in ethnic segregation III: Segregation outcomes. *Urban Geography, 32*(4), 589–605.

Key, V. O. (1949). *Southern politics in state and nation.* New York: Knopf.

Kiang, L., Perreira, K. M., & Fuligni, A. J. (2011). Ethnic label use in adolescents from traditional and non-traditional immigrant communities. *Journal of Youth Adolescence, 40*, 719–29.

Lewin, A. C., Stier, H., & Caspi-Dror, D. (2006). The place of opportunity: Community and individual determinants of poverty among Jews and Arabs in Israel. *Research in Social Stratification and Mobility, 24*, 177–91.

Markert, J. (2010). The changing face of racial discrimination: Hispanics as the dominant minority in the USA—a new application of power-threat theory. *Critical Sociology, 36*, 307–327.

Massey, D. S. (2007). *Categorically unequal: The American stratification system.* New York: Russell Sage Foundation.

Novak, M. (1972). *The rise of the unmeltable ethnics: Politics and culture in the seventies.* NY: The Macmillan Company.

Sáenz, R. (1997). Ethnic concentration and Chicano poverty: A comparative approach. *Social Science Research, 26*, 205–228.

Sáenz, R., Cready, C. M., & Morales, M. C. (2007). Adios Aztlan: Mexican American outmigration from the Southwest. In L. M. Lobao, G. Hoods, & A. R. Tickamyer (Eds.), *The sociology of spatial inequality* (pp. 189–214). Albany, NY: State University of New York Press.

Schlueter, E., & Scheepers, P. (2010). The relationship between outgroup size and anti-outgroup attitudes: A theoretical synthesis and empirical test of group threat- and intergroup contact theory. *Social Science Research, 36*, 285–295.

Siordia, C. (2011). Sociospatial inequality: A multilevel and geo-spatial analysis of Latino poverty. (Doctoral dissertation). Texas A&M University, College Station, Texas. Available at: http://gateway.proquest.com/openurl%3furl_ver=Z39.88-2004%26res_dat=xri:pqdiss%26rft_val_fmt=info:ofi/fmt:kev:mtx:dissertation%26rft_dat=xri:pqdiss:3500095.

Tavernise, S. (2011, September 13). Soaring poverty casts spotlight on 'Lost Decade' The New York Times. Available at: http://relooney.fatcow.com/0_New_11194.pdf

Wang, Q. (2010). The earnings effect of ethnic labour market concentration under multi-racial metropolitan contexts in the United States. *Tijdschrift voor Economische en Sociale Geografie, 101*(2), 161–176.

Yzaguirre, R., Suro, R., Ajami, F., Daniels, R., Jacoby, T., Buchanan, P., et al., (2004). Huntington and Hispanics. *Foreign Policy, 142*, 4, 6, 8–10, 12–13, 84–91.

CHAPTER 6

# RURAL LATINOS

## An Assessment of Evolving Conditions

**Refugio I. Rochín**
*University of California, Davis and Santa Cruz*

This chapter brings attention to the increasing significance of Latinos in rural America. It goes beyond the stereotypes of the Latino foreign-born as undocumented immigrants who are poorly educated and employed primarily as farm workers. While there is some validity to these characterizations, these depictions overlook the fact that rural places are being transformed from small towns with mostly English-speaking non-Hispanic White and Black residents, to diverse, enriched communities where Spanish is common and new cultural dimensions are being forged.

Rural Latinos are found as educators, police and firemen, service providers, owner-operators of all kinds of businesses, local leaders, and, without a doubt, the fastest growing population of rural America. They reside in every state and niche with various degrees of integration and acculturation. Nonetheless, the continuing growth of Latinos portends both positive and negative situations. Their newness and growth comes amidst national issues of unchecked immigration, rural unemployment, environmental health, and the provision of schooling and services for English-language-challenged newcomers.

*The Economic Status of the Hispanic Population*, pages 81–93
Copyright © 2013 by Information Age Publishing
All rights of reproduction in any form reserved.

Several reports and academic research, particularly from the 1980s and 1990s (decades when many Latino issues found today escalated) are discussed in parts of this chapter (a more extensive list can be obtained from the author). This extant research reminds us of the apparent need to improve our knowledge of rural communities and conditions where Latinos live.

## RURAL AMERICA IN TRANSITION

It is important to note that "Rural America" is both a concept of geography and a way of life within the United States. There is no precise or accepted definition for this term owing to America's evolution from an agrarian society (roughly speaking from the time of the American Revolution to 1900) into a nation of super-sized metropolitan cities like New York, Los Angeles, and Chicago. Nonetheless, American scholars have continued to study the nation in terms of rural and urban people. To measure the populations and densities of rural and urban America, the U.S. Census Bureau has adopted the concepts of "non-metropolitan" and "metropolitan" areas, respectively.

The distinction is basic: metropolitan areas hold millions of people in relatively small terrain—constituting population centers of 50,000 or more. Non-metro areas hold smaller clusters of people in huge geographic areas. This distinction highlights the fact that a relatively small population in rural America has control or oversight of major spaces, encompassing the U.S. interior, border frontiers and the vast terrain of natural resources.

Nonetheless, from 1980 to 2000, according to William Kandel and John Cromartie (2004), the non-metro "rural" Latino population doubled in number while other population groups diminished in absolute number. Immigration and relatively larger households increased the population of rural Latinos at a rapid rate. Latinos also dispersed into non-traditional geographic regions; for example, these authors reported that by 2000, over half of non-metro Latinos resided outside of their traditional Southwestern settlement areas. In the 1990s, according to Kandel and Cromartie, Latino population growth prevented overall population decline in over 100 non-metro rural counties, many of which lost population during the 1980s.

Rural Latinos also introduced challenges to rural communities in a number of ways. Kandel and Cromartie found that Latinos in many of these rapidly growing non-metro counties were recent immigrants (including the undocumented) who had below-average education levels and lacked English-language proficiency. These authors noted that these demographic changes: "…increased the visibility of Hispanics in many new regions of rural America whose population has long been dominated by non-Hispanic Whites. Yet, within smaller geographic areas, the level of residential separation between them increased…." Kandel and Cromartie also pointed out that Latinos' settlement patterns warrant policy attention because they "...affect the well-being of both Hispanics and rural communities themselves."

## AGRICULTURE AND LATINO WORKERS

Agriculture and farming have been the basic foundations for Latino growth and settlement in rural America. Today, agro-industrialization and its adherents, support liberal immigration policies but reject unions. Contemporary immigration from Mexico has continued steadily because of farmers' demands for larger and larger numbers of low-cost workers. As indicated by L. Calvin and Phillip Martin (2010), this labors' hard work and patterns of migration and settlement produce a situation for farmers to depend on Mexican labor, mostly unauthorized immigrants.

Latinos have moved into and joined the workforce of rural areas, particularly where farms have "industrialized" to the point that large scale farms for many products (especially fruits, vegetables, and processed meats and vegetables) have generated a strong, large demand of low-cost workers. Being successful as producers of low-cost produce, agro-industrialization has been a boon for migrant workers and especially for those who are immigrants.

Large-scale producers assure their supply of labor with allies in Congress who support the employment of "temporary guest workers." Guest workers with temporary visas (H2-IA) date back to 1941 with the Bracero Program, which started as an alliance between the United States and Mexico to have food security during World War II. Bracero workers (field workers) were drafted in Mexico, employed during peak harvest and processing periods in the United States, and returned to Mexico during the slow periods of growing crops and products. This program made it possible for both governments to supply workers at timely periods and to have the workers return to Mexico during post-harvest periods (see Philip Martin et al., 1996).

This system was perpetuated by increasing pools of Mexican workers desiring to work in the United States, far beyond the actual demand for workers at higher wages. Farmers and their proponents in Congress locally opposed funding public services needed to integrate immigrants and their children into the mainstream of American life. They succeeded in hiring workers, despite the end of the Bracero Program and the rise of immigrant barriers between the United States and Mexico.

The end of the Bracero program in 1964 was partly attributed to Ernesto Galarza's exposé of this program, *Merchants of Labor: The Bracero Story*. He was born on August 15, 1905 in Jalcocotan, Nayrit, Mexico and immigrated to the United States in 1911. And while the Bracero Program was largely concentrated in America's Southwest, Latinos now have notable populations in the Midwest, Southern, and Eastern counties. In essence they fill into places as White and Blacks move out. Rural Latinos also adjust to closing plants in manufacturing and retail economic business sectors. During this transition, Latinos struggle but show resilience against economic changes. They also settle with relatively low education levels, weak English-language proficiency, and undocumented status (e.g., Millard & Chapa, 2004; Cobas, 1986, 1987).

## THE CHANGING FACE OF RURAL AMERICA

Since the passage of The Immigration Reform and Control Act of 1986, studies, such as those by Lourdes Gouveia (2006) and Refugio Rochín and Monica Castillo (1993), have covered U.S. immigration and the flows of Mexican and Latino workers into rural America. They show a changing face in rural America and identify several communities of new rural Latino workers, especially in California, Texas, Florida, and the American Midwest, where agro-industrial production includes large pools of workers, such as in meatpacking and processing.

More recent studies have depicted how rural Latinos are concentrating in the East and South where out-migration of non-Hispanic Whites and Blacks has continued. In those places, Latinos have moved into small communities with all kinds of new jobs and employment. Latinos are generating a new dynamic for housing and business as well as a questionable situation for health, schooling, and language issues.

In general, rural Latinos have proven to be resilient in terms of buying homes, addressing schooling, and absorbing new residents who are largely self-employed and equally adept of creating new forms of work and employment. Because of Latino workers, rural America has a way of producing low-cost, quality products as well as sustainable communities, even where Latinos become the majority of rural towns and places. There is also an apparent ebb and flow of Latino workers, who sometimes enter rural America as farm workers but shift quickly to work in construction, services, and small business with skill and determination. This versatility can be considered a positive response to changing economic conditions and community well-being.

## THE ADVENT OF "RURAL LATINIZATION" IN CALIFORNIA

One of the first studies to show a pattern of "rural Latinization" was conducted by Monica Castillo in 1991. She set out to research California's "rural *colonias*" to see if areas with relatively large concentrations of Latino farm workers produced healthy, viable communities. In her study she gathered 1980 Census data on 148 small rural places in California. Empirically analyzing socioeconomic conditions, she found that rural *colonias* as well as small communities in which Latinos comprised the majority appeared to lag behind the rest of California, including other small rural communities. To quote: "The study establishes that rural *colonias* are relatively disadvantaged in terms of private sector activities, enjoying only the most minimal development of local business establishments which provide basic goods and services (e.g., food, clothing, and transportation)."

Several questions follow from Castillo's findings. What happens as Latinos move in to rural places? How does this process of Latino settlement come about? Have rural communities improved the livelihood of their residents? Are they better off than before or facing serious needs and problems?

In addressing these questions, Elaine Allensworth and Refugio Rochín (1996 and 1999) examined the changing demographics from 1980 to 1990 of 126 rural communities in California, using U.S. Census data to compare and contrast conditions over a decade. The communities of their study had populations of fewer than 20,000 residents in 1980 (small by California standards) and a labor force of 15% or more employed in agriculture and farms.

Their data are shown in Figure 6.1, where each community is identified on the horizontal access, ranging from the smallest community (Citrus) to the largest community in 1980 (Century). In the figure, there are four things to note. First, there is a dot and a box for each of the communities (a few communities are named within the chart to illustrate examples). Second, the horizontal axis spreads out the communities from a low to a high growth in total population between 1980 and 1990, and the vertical axis measures the absolute magnitude of population change of each community in that decade. Third, the top curve of dots shows the growth in overall population of each community and the lower curve of boxes shows the growth of non-Hispanic Whites of each community. Fourth, from left to right, the most changed communities in terms of Latino population shares can be determined.

To understand Figure 6.1, notice the community at the far left with negative growth. This community, Citrus, lost 4,003 non-Latino residents and added 1,307 Latino residents from 1980 to 1990, so its total population change was –2,969. At the other extreme, is Cathedral City that gained 25,955 new residents between 1980 and 1990, of which 10,082 (almost half) were Latino? Gonzalez, the community to which the arrow points in the figure, is representative of the majority of rural California communities. This community experienced a slight decrease in non-Hispanic Whites (–90), but an increase in overall population (+1,769) due to the increase in the number of its Latino residents (+1,859). Notice that in over half of the communities depicted, there was no growth in non-

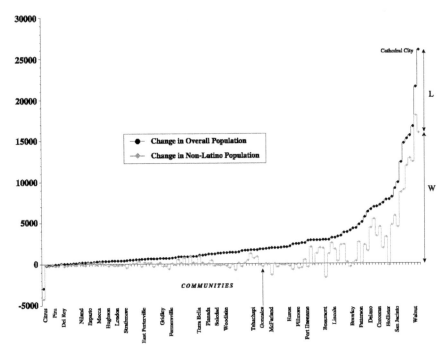

**Figure 6.1** Population Growth of Rural California Communities (1980-1990). *Source:* Adapted from Allensworth and Rochín (1996). *Note:* Reported in absolute numbers; n = 126 rural communities.

Hispanic Whites, despite an increase in total population. Thus, in these 126 communities, changes in Latino population accounted, on average, for over 100% of the population growth from 1980 to 1990, making up for absolute losses in non-Hispanic Whites. Without additions in Latinos, the overall population in most of these rural communities would have decreased in absolute number.

When summarizing such changes, Allensworth and Rochín identified the following patterns of "rural Latinization".

1.  There were 15 communities that experienced large gains in non-Hispanic Whites (greater than 50% growth) as well as comparable gains in Latino population of more than 50%. There were 45 communities that experienced increases (up to 50%) in non-Hispanic Whites while simultaneously experiencing gains in Latino population.

2.  There were 64 communities that lost non-Hispanic Whites in absolute amounts and there were two communities that lost population, although these communities were relatively small and the loss in

their populations was less than a 100 people overall. These losses, however, were clearly offset by the influx of Latinos. Overall, all but two communities had population growth.

Allensworth and Rochín further examined the changes in socioeconomic well-being associated with the changing demographics of communities using various empirical techniques. This analysis excluded the two communities that lost population and divided the communities into three groups. The first group consisted of those 62 communities in which the Latino population increased, while the non-Hispanic White population decreased or remained the same. The second group of communities increased in population size between both ethnic groups, but the Latino population increased by a larger number. The third group of communities consisted of those going through significant increases in the size of both populations.

Their findings, contained in Table 6.1, show significant differences in well-being across these three sets of communities cross-sectionally in terms of data for 1990 (Panel A) as well as over time (from 1980 to 1990, Panel B). To illustrate, the first row of Table 6.1 shows large differences in poverty

**TABLE 6.1 Comparison of Community Well-Being by Groups with Noted Changes in Latino and Non-Latino Populations from 1980 to 1990**

| Indicators of Well-Being | Group 1: Decrease In Non-Latinos/ Increase in Latinos (*n* = 62) | Group 2: Small Increase in Non-Latinos/ Large Increase in Latinos (*n* = 32) | Group 3: Similar Increase in Non-Latinos and Latinos (*n* = 29) |
|---|---|---|---|
| **Panel A: Cross-sectional (1990)** | | | |
| % Community in poverty | 26.6% | 18.4% | 13.8% |
| Median income | $24,319 | $24,625 | $33,817 |
| % High school graduates (over 25) | 39.4% | 60.4% | 65.1% |
| % College graduates (over 25) | 5.5% | 9.9% | 10.8% |
| **Panel B: Change between 1980–1990** | | | |
| Change in % in poverty | 12.9 | 7.8 | 4.1 |
| Change in median income | $10.33 | $10,896 | $17,514 |
| Change in % high school graduates | 0.40% | 6.30% | 9.90% |
| Change in % college graduates | –0.60% | 1.30% | 1.90% |

*Source:* Adapted from Allensworth and Rochín (1996).
*Note:* The actual sample sizes used to estimate these characteristics were smaller than the total group sizes shown due to data availability; see Allensworth and Rochín (1996) for more details.

rates between the three types of communities in 1990, based on Latino and non-Hispanic White population-size changes. Communities that experienced decreases in non-Hispanic Whites (Group 1) had poverty rates that were 8% higher than those of communities where the ethnic composition changed and were 13% higher than for communities in which the ethnic populations grew more evenly. Hence, poverty seems to be tied to both increases in Latino population and decreases in non-Hispanic Whites. This finding is supported by the results shown in Row 6, which compare changes in poverty with changes in population. Communities that experienced decreases in non-Hispanic Whites experienced significantly greater increases in poverty rates between 1980 and 1990.

The second row shows a slightly different pattern in terms of median income. Groups 1 and 2 both had significantly lower median incomes than communities in which Latino and non-Hispanic Whites grew at similar rates. However, the median incomes of the first two types of communities were not significantly different from each other. The same pattern occurs when we consider changes in median incomes from 1980 to 1990 (seventh row). The first two types of communities experienced median income growth of about $10,000, while communities in which Latino and non-Hispanic Whites grew at similar rates had median income growth of about $17,000.

The pattern for high school completion is different from the patterns for both poverty and median income. Communities in which non-Hispanic Whites decreased in the 1980s show significantly smaller percentages of high school graduates than communities in which non-Hispanic Whites grew, regardless of changes in ethnic composition. On average, only 39% of adults in communities that lost non-Hispanic Whites had graduated from high school, while over 60% of the adults in communities that gained this population had high school degrees. The same pattern holds by noting changes in the percentage of adults with high school degrees between 1980 and 1990. In the former communities, the change in the percentage of adults with high school degrees between 1980 and 1990 was less than 1%. The latter communities experienced average increases in the percentage of adults with high school degrees of 6–9%. Similar patterns emerge regarding the percentage of adults with college degrees.

Although community conditions were worse in places experiencing the exodus of non-Hispanic Whites, an increase in the Latino population of a community was also associated with positive economic conditions. These improvements were evident in terms of the second and third categories of communities. In fact, throughout rural California, places which added significant numbers of both groups improved in terms of family income, employment, and education in the 1980s. But when communities lost non-

Hispanic Whites and added Latinos in their place, there was an associated decline in the indicators of social well-being.

## RURAL LATINO ENTREPRENEURS

Are Latino residents relatively more entrepreneurial within *colonias*, taking advantage of language and culture as driving forces for business? What types of businesses are present in *colonias*? Or, are *colonias* generally deprived of entrepreneurs and the prospects for local development? A 1998 study by Refugio Rochín, Rogelio Sáenz, Steve Hampton, and Bea Calo examined the general conditions of *colonias* and Latino entrepreneurs (the self-employed) in rural California, using data from the U.S. Censuses of Population and Economic Businesses, covering 1970–1990. They developed a database of over 145 communities with populations of 2,000 to 20,000 in 1980 as a marker from which to compare business activity and socio-demographic changes over time. Census data were also supplemented by California data on factors like taxes, revenues, and school districts. In short, the results from this study both confirmed and contradicted some of the hypothesis of extant literature regarding Latino entrepreneurs.

Striking differences between non-Hispanic White and Latino entrepreneurs in rural California were found by these authors, especially with regards to the *colonia* conditions, the relative employment options for residents, and their levels of education. They noticed that self-employment among Latinos was closely correlated with structural conditions. That is, the higher the proportion of Latinos in a community, the greater the self-employment of Latinos in relative terms. Structuralist conditions, however, related to fewer economic opportunities for residents: higher unemployment, higher concentrations of workers in agriculture, limited educational attainment among Latinos, and general economic deprivation within *colonias*. All combined, their study found that Latino entrepreneurs were relatively more evident in *colonias* with high proportions of Latinos, but their customers were generally poorer. To a degree, these findings suggest that *colonia* entrepreneurs might be self-employed as part of their own means for survival.

Bea Calo (1995) completed a general overview of Latino entrepreneurship among rural places in California. With data from the 1990 decennial census, Calo identified and compared rural Latinos from others. Criteria used by Calo to determine "rural" was derived from a non-standard geographical entity Public Use Microdata Area (PUMA). Each PUMA represents an area with a total population of at least 100,000; a PUMA considers a rural community to be in a non-metropolitan county or in a metropolitan county with a density of less than 1,000 people per square mile. Of California's 198 PUMAs, 44 met the study's operational definition of "rural."

Based on this sample, Calo found that 9% of the rural Chicano households in 1990 had someone who was full-time self-employed. This is in line with estimates from the Bureau of Labor Statistics (1991), showing that, on average, self-employment of 8.6% of the workforce in 1989. Of the 865 Latino entrepreneurs in Calo's study, 620 were self-employed on a full-time basis, while the other 245 were also wage-employed and involved in entrepreneurial activities only on a part-time basis. Other findings from this study revealed that self-employed Latinos tended to be older, more educated, more likely to be married, more assimilated, and wealthier than their wage-earning counterparts. It should be noted that, although Calo's findings are unique and useful for understanding self-employed Latinos in rural areas in California, the findings do not necessarily relate to the structural and cultural conditions of rural *colonias*.

## CONCLUSION

Rural Latinos are gaining ground and establishing themselves in productive, gainful ways. Latino population growth is seen to fill jobs, fill houses, expand the consumer base, and rebuild a waning population or form a population base to keep cities from disappearing. But it would be a mistake to think of them as living an idyllic life. There are troubling signs for many. Studies continue to find that communities with proportionately higher concentrations of Latinos tend to have greater poverty, lower median incomes, and smaller proportions of residents with high school or college degrees.

Latino population growth in rural areas is blamed for deterioration of neighborhoods, declining real earnings through wage competition, and for the incentives leading to further restructuring, both in agriculture and manufacturing. According to the subordination thesis, increasing minority population can accentuate competition for particular jobs, so that minorities build a common ground to the exclusion of others. Such a perspective is consistent with a neoclassical economic view of labor supply and demand, that a constantly increasing supply of low-wage labor lowers wages for both new and established migrants. As a result, immigration has been blamed for the low earnings and unstable employment of rural Latinos.

Recent studies have shown that Latino spatial concentrations can have negative effects on local communities, slightly increasing under-employment, poverty, and public assistance use, although raising mean incomes. In other words, the employment opportunities and earnings of low-skill workers are slightly reduced with increased Latino concentration, although the prospects for economic growth of the community as a whole (especially those who can take advantage of cheap and abundant labor) are increased.

Ethnic and class divisions between local non-Hispanic White elites and Latinos have resulted in fractured communities, within which the traditional elite has tried to develop the local economy not through residents' demands for social equity, but through residential and economic segregation. Furthermore, there is reason to believe that the non-Hispanic White exodus from many of the rural places where Latinos are settling is due, at least in part, to anti-immigrant, anti-Latino, or anti-farm-worker feelings.

Rural community news articles point to increased ethnic conflict between non-Hispanic Whites and Latinos, as the Latino population increases in size (see Millard & Chapa, 2004). In some communities, non-Hispanic Whites seem to leave as the Latino population moves in, especially in old neighborhoods. What follows are distinct ethnic neighborhoods, with most of the community resources invested in the non-Hispanic Whites' side of town, and conflicts erupting with charges of racism and discrimination. Furthermore, the hypothesis that increasing minority representation in a place encourages out-migration of majority group members is not new. "White flight" from urban areas has been consistently blamed on non-Hispanic Whites' fear of integration with Blacks and their fear that property values will decline with greater numbers of minority residents.

Places undergoing this rapid turnover have had to confront sudden demands for housing, education, health care, social services, and crime prevention. In most of these places, available housing has been inadequate, overcrowded, and dangerous. Lack of health insurance for Latino workers and difficulties in affording co-payments among the insured have led to large inadequate prenatal care, problems with tuberculosis, gaps in child immunization, and deficient dental care. Related increases in school enrollments have brought about the need for bilingual and English-as-a-Second-Language instruction. However, it is difficult to find and attract qualified bilingual teachers to remote places.

Latino teenagers find it especially difficult to gain enough English-language skills or social confidence to be successful in high school, and so have problems with truancy, pregnancy, dropping out, and gang development, implying worsening conditions for future generations. School turnover is relatively high in meatpacking towns, paralleling that of the plants. Language translation has become an expensive issue for courts, schools, and social service providers.

On top of these matters, recent research by Victor Garcia and Laura Gonzalez (2009) has identified problems with the transnational communities of Mexican workers. They present findings on drug use and the emergence of drug use culture in Mexican migrant streams. Garcia and Gonzalez examined the manner in which transnational migration and drug trafficking organizations are contributing to a growing drug problem in these communities. They found that transnational migrants and returning immigrants, including deported workers, introduce drugs and drug use practices, and contribute to the creation of a drug-use culture with the communities.

## REFERENCES

Allensworth, E., & Rochín, R. I. (1999). The Mexicanization of rural California: A socio-demographic analysis, 1980–1997. *Research Report, 11.* The Julian Samora Research Institute, Michigan State University, East Lansing.

Allensworth, E., & Rochín, R. I. (1996). White exodus, Latino re-population and community well-being: Trends in California's rural communities. *JSRI Research Report, 13.* The Julian Samora Research Institute, Michigan State University, East Lansing, Mich. June 1996.

Calo, B. V. (1995). Chicano entrepreneurship in rural California: An empirical analysis. PhD dissertation in Agricultural Economics, University of California, Davis. Funded under the auspices of USDA/National Research Initiative Grant to R. Saenz and R.I. Rochín.

Calvin, L., & Martin, P. (2010). The U.S. produce industry and labor: Facing the future in a global economy. *USDA. Economic Research Report, 11.* Available at http://www.ers.usda.gov/Publications/ERR106/.

Castillo, M. D. (1991). California's rural *colonias*: A study of disadvantaged communities with high concentrations of Latinos. M.S. Degree Thesis in International Agricultural Development, University of California, Davis. 226 pp.

Cobas, J. A. (1986). Paths to self-employment among immigrants: An analysis of four interpretations. *Sociological Perspectives, 29,* 101–120.

Cobas, J. A. (1987). Ethnic enclaves and middleman minorities: Alternative strategies of immigrant adaptation? *Sociological Perspectives, 30(2),* 143–161.

Garcia, V., & Gonzalez, L. (2009). Labor migration, drug trafficking organizations, and drug use: Major challenges for transnational communities in Mexico. *Urban Anthropology, 38,* 2–42.

Gouveia, L. (2006). Nebraska's responses to immigration. In G. Anrig, Jr. & T. Wang (Eds), *Immigration's new frontiers: Experiences from the emerging gateway states* (pp. 143–198). New York: Century Foundation Press.

Kandel, W., & Cromartie, J. (2004). New patterns of Hispanic settlement in rural America. A Report from the Economic Research Service, No. 99.

Martin, P. L., Huffman, W., Emerson, R., Taylor, J. E., & Rochín, R. I. (1996). *Immigration reform and U.S. agriculture.* University of California, Agriculture & Natural Resources.

Millard, A. V., & Chapa., J. (2004). *Apple pie and enchiladas: Latino newcomers in the rural Midwest,* With Catalina Burillo, Ken R. Crane, Isidore Flores, Maríalena D. Jefferds, Eileen Diaz McConnell, Refugio I. Rochín, and Rogelio Sáenz. Austin: University of Texas Press.

Rochín, R. I., & Castillo, M. D. (1993). Immigration, *colonia* formation, and Latino poor in rural California. *Occasional Paper Series No.93-1.* The Tomas Rivera Center: Claremont, *2*, 204–223.

Rochín, R. I., Saenz, R., Hampton, S., & Calo, B. (1998). *Colonias* and Chicano/a entrepreneurs in rural California, *JSRI Research Report #16,* The Julian Samora Research Institute, Michigan State University.

CHAPTER 7

# THE ECONOMY AND LATINOS

## Trying to Find "Affordable Care" with High Medical Costs and the Economic Recession

**Jillian Medeiros**
*University of New Mexico*

**Gabriel Sanchez**
*University of New Mexico*

Healthcare costs in the United States have been rapidly rising in recent years, with health expenditures exceeding \$2.2 trillion in 2007 (Henry J. Kaiser Family Foundation, 2009a). That same year, Kaiser estimated that healthcare spending was about \$7,421 per resident, accounting for 16.2% of the U.S. Gross Domestic Product, such that the United States has one of the highest health-spending rankings among industrialized countries. Rising healthcare costs have had major implications at the individual level as well, with some families having to cut back on basic necessities such as food and electricity, and in extreme cases their homes, to afford healthcare and insurance (Fletcher, 2008; National Coalition on Health

*The Economic Status of the Hispanic Population*, pages 95–112
Copyright © 2013 by Information Age Publishing
All rights of reproduction in any form reserved.

Care, 2009). Unfortunately, these cases are not isolated incidents, as many Americans cannot keep pace with the soaring costs of health insurance, and an increasing number of Americans are living without access to healthcare every day. For example, in 2007, 45 million non-elderly people in the United States lacked health coverage, and since 2000 the number of non-elderly uninsured has grown by eight million (Henry J. Kaiser Family Foundation, 2008).

The impact of rising healthcare costs has been compounded by a growing number of employers deciding to cut back on offering insurance benefits at the same time that average premiums are rising. In fact, since 1999 the average premium costs for family coverage have increased by a robust 119% (Henry J. Kaiser Family Foundation/Health Research/ Educational Trust, 2008). Rising healthcare costs combined with the recent economic crisis have resulted in a growing number of families being faced with the prospect of having to ration or forgo medical care in order to afford other critical resources such as rent and food. A recent Kaiser Health Tracking Poll found that more than half (53%) of Americans indicated that their families had cut back on medical care in the past 12 months due to cost concerns (Henry J. Kaiser Family Foundation, 2009b).

Banthin, Cunningham, Bernard, and Didem (2008) found similar patterns when analyzing the financial burden of healthcare from 2001 to 2004. Their analysis demonstrated that rising out-of-pocket expenses and stagnant incomes increased the health-spending financial burden on families during that time. By 2004, they estimated that 45.4 million people lived in families with high burdens—an increase of almost 6 million people from 2001. The two principal factors driving these increases were increases in health insurance premiums and out-of-pocket spending on healthcare services. After adjusting for inflation, they estimated that out-of-pocket spending for premiums and services rose from $553 to an alarming $3,211 over the four-year period.

While it seems clear that the rising costs of health insurance and healthcare more generally have negatively impacted American families, we know little about how the rapidly rising costs are affecting one of the most at-risk populations in terms of healthcare and access, the Latino community.[1] This population warrants attention as the federal healthcare reform debates heat up, particularly because Latinos have the highest uninsured rates and the lowest percentage of people with employer-provided health insurance when compared with Non-Latino Whites, African Americans, Asian/Pacific Islanders, American Indian/Alaska Natives, and multiracial persons (James, Thomas, Lillie-Blanton, & Garfield, 2007). Moreover, the U.S. Census Bureau reported that 30.7% of the Latino population in 2010 was not covered by health insurance, compared to 11.7% of the non-Hispanic White population.

Because Latinos appear to be a vulnerable population in terms of health-care and access, we focus our analysis on the impact of the current high costs of healthcare on the health-seeking behavior (e.g., skipping medical visits, not filling prescriptions or relying on alternatives) of Latino registered voters, as well as how these costs have affected the personal finances of this population. Given that Latinos represent a relatively large (and growing) portion of the U.S. population, health problems of the Latino community have become more of a national issue and concern.

## RISING MEDICAL COSTS, UNDER-INSURANCE, AND FINANCIAL STRAIN IN THE UNITED STATES

The rising healthcare costs in the United States have led to an environment in which health insurance alone is insufficient to cover Americans' healthcare needs (Raiz, 2006). Insurance policies with substantial cost-sharing measures have been shown to undermine access to care and diminish family finances in ways similar to lacking insurance all together (Schoen, Collins, Kriss, & Doty, 2008). That is, families that experience *under-insurance* bear financial burdens that prohibit them from accessing care. Under-insurance refers to the state of having health insurance but the insurance not adequately protecting one from high medical expenses. Schoen and colleagues (2008) define an individual as being under-insured if at least one of the following indicators is met:

1. Out-of-pocket medical expenses amount to 10% of income or more.
2. Among low-income adults (below 200% of federal poverty level) medical expenses amount to at least 5% of income.
3. Deductibles equal or exceed 5% of income.

Based on these indicators of cost-exposure relative to income, Schoen et al., found that as of 2007, 25 million Americans aged 19–64 were under-insured. When combined with the segment of the population that lacks insurance, they further estimated that 42% of U.S. adults were under-insured or uninsured in 2007, which suggests that a large segment of the population is vulnerable to rising healthcare costs. They also found that the number of under-insured adults had risen 60% since 2003.

Additionally, researchers have found that having private medical insurance does not protect people from being under-insured and from rising healthcare costs. For example, J. Banthin et al., found that people with private insurance experienced high financial burdens and under-insurance in 2001–2004, due to rising out-of-pocket healthcare expenses and stagnant incomes. Moreover, ethnicity was found to have an impact on under-insurance rates. For example, as noted above, Latinos are more likely to be under-insured when compared to non-Hispanic Whites. Therefore, a large portion of Americans are experiencing under-insurance, with Latinos facing higher rates of under-insurance than non-Hispanic Whites.

Scholars have found a relationship between lack of insurance and under-insurance rates and economic strain. While it is intuitive that a high percentage of uninsured adults report high rates of financial stress due to medical bills, it is somewhat surprising that a nearly identical percentage (nearly half) of the under-insured population has difficulty paying medical bills (Schoen et al., 2008, p. 305). Across socioeconomic groups, the burdens of rising healthcare costs in the early 2000s were highest among the poor (53%) and low-income individuals with private insurance (37.4%) (Banthin et al., 2008). Out-of-pocket spending for both premiums and services appeared to be driving the financial burden for these two groups. Specifically, 30.1% of Americans below the poverty line and 21.9% of low-income Americans incurred financial burdens from the costs of premiums, compared with 39.7% of the poor and 10.4% of low-income Americans who incurred high burdens solely from out-of-pocket spending on services in 2004 (Banthin et al., 2008). Low-income adults with public coverage such as Medicaid and Medicare also reported significant financial burdens. For instance, in 2005, 25% of adults with public coverage spent more than 10% of their income on medical care (Schoen, Doty, Collins, & Holmgren, 2005).

Extant research also finds that rising healthcare costs have contributed to bankruptcy for many Americans (Himmelstein, Warren, Thorne, & Woolhandler, 2005, 2009). For example, 62.1% of all bankruptcies in 2007 were due to medical costs, with 92% of these medical-based cases having significant medical debts of more than $5,000, or 10% of their pretax family income (Himmelstein et al., 2009). From 2001 to 2007 the share of bankruptcies attributed to medical costs and problems rose by 49.6% (Himmelstein et al., 2009). Interestingly, those who declared bankruptcy due to medical costs tended to be middle-class, well-educated homeowners who had health insurance. Some people with continuous medical insurance were under-insured, and thus had to pay thousands of dollars for out-of-pocket medical care costs. Others possessed private insurance coverage but lost it when they became too ill to work (Himmelstein et al., 2009). Overall, previous research indicates that current high medical costs have led to severe financial stress for American families.

The recent under-insurance and socioeconomic trends reviewed here suggest that having health insurance may not provide adequate protection from rising healthcare costs. We therefore control for both income and insurance coverage in our analysis to determine if having health insurance helps insulate Latino registered voters from the economic impact and health-related response related to healthcare expenses.

## LATINOS: A VULNERABLE POPULATION

As aforementioned, Latinos disproportionately lack health insurance compared with other racial and ethnic groups in the United States. Although they have similar employment rates as other groups, one of the main reasons for Latinos' health-insurance under-coverage is that their jobs tend to be less likely to offer such coverage (James et al., 2007). According to a recent Gallup Poll, only 28.3% of Hispanics had employer-based insurance in 2011 (a share which had declined since 2008), compared to 49.2% of Whites, and 38.1% of African-Americans (Mendes, 2012).

Several other factors also help to explain why Latinos disproportionately lack employer-based insurance, including the fact that four out of five unauthorized immigrants (who have difficulties in securing employment with formal medical benefits) are Latino.[2] The estimated 6.5 million unauthorized Mexican immigrants comprise the majority (58%) of the unauthorized immigrant population in the United States, and another 2.6 million non-Mexican Latin Americans account for 23% of this population (Passel & Cohn, 2011).

Latinos' under-representation among the college educated is another factor, as individuals with more education are more likely to have health insurance (e.g., Carrillo, Trevino, Betancourt, & Coustasse, 2001). For example, according to our estimates using the 2010 American Community Survey, only 41.5% of Latinos ages 25–64 with less than a high school diploma had some type of health insurance coverage. Furthermore, among Latinos in this age range with a high school education but no college, 57.0% had health insurance. However, 79.3% of Latinos with a four-year college degree (but no additional schooling) had health insurance, as did 86.7% of those with more than a college degree. Hence, in 2010, the health insurance coverage rate among Latinos with a college degree or higher was twice as high as for Latinos with less than a high school education. Clearly, having a higher level of education increases the likelihood of having health insurance.

Additional employment-based explanations include the fact that Latinos are more likely to work in industries that do not provide benefits, such as agriculture, service, mining, domestic service, and construction (Carrillo et al., 2001). Finally, Latino employees who work in small businesses are also half as likely to have employer coverage and twice as likely to be uninsured as non-Hispanic White workers (Carrillo et al., 2001).

Studies on managed care systems show that Latinos enroll in these services at a lower rate when compared with other racial and ethnic groups. For example, a study conducted in Florida, Tennessee, and Texas showed that among low-income groups, only 55% of Latinos were enrolled in managed care, compared with 72 % of African Americans and 63% of non-Hispanic Whites (Leigh, Lillie-Blanton, Martinez, & Collins, 1999). Latinos tend to lack coverage through Medicaid as well. The Personal Responsibility and Work Opportunity Reconciliation Act (PRWORA) of 1996 caused many Latinos not to enroll with Medicaid because they did not understand the process, did not know they were eligible, and feared being deported by the Immigration and Naturalization Service (INS) for enrolling in the Medicaid program (Carrillo et al., 2001; Hagan, Rodriguez, Capps, & Kabiri., 2003; Kullgren, 2003). The effect of the PRWORA is that many Latinos dropped out or did not enroll in Medicaid. For example, in New York City, where a significant amount of the Medicaid population is Latino, Medicaid enrollment fell by 12% (200,000) after the PRWORA was implemented (1995–1999) (Carrillo et al., 2001). In sum, Latinos' lack of healthcare coverage stems from a variety of factors.

Beyond lacking health insurance, Latinos encounter other barriers to healthcare access, including the lack of Latino medical providers, few culturally competent providers, language barriers, and sparse medical care facilities in their communities (e.g., Valdez, Giachello, Rodriguez-Trias, Gomez, & De la Rocha 1993a; Derose & Baker, 2000; Weinack & Kraus, 2000; Carillo et al., 2001; Fiscell, Franks, Doescher, & Saver, 2002). These barriers combined with a lack of insurance have led to Latinos utilizing healthcare services less than the general population. For example, Latinos have been found to be less likely to receive prenatal care, mammograms, Papanicolaou tests, and blood cholesterol checks when compared with non-Hispanic Whites (National Center for Health Statistics, 2000).

Considering that Latinos appear to be a vulnerable population in terms of healthcare access and utilization, it is critical to examine how medical costs affect the health-seeking behavior of this population and their personal finances. Unfortunately, there is little research analyzing how medical costs affect the health behavior of Latinos or their finances. One survey conducted by the Kaiser Family Foundation, however, found that Latinos feel the cost of insurance and medical care is a major problem, more problematic in fact than not having enough health providers in their communities or not getting medical care because of racial discrimination (Lillie-Blanton, Brodi, Rowland, Altman, & McIntosh, 2000).

The rising cost of healthcare likely impacts Latinos regardless of coverage status, as earlier studies suggest that Latinos covered by health insurance found it difficult to pay for healthcare services. For example, two decades ago, Latinos with Medicaid appear to have had difficulties in locating providers willing to accept the low payment schedules, and Latinos with private insurance were burdened with higher out-of-pocket costs associated with healthcare (e.g., Valdez et al., 1993a; Valdez, Morgenstern, Brown, Wyn, Wang, & Cumberland, 1993b). However, we do not know how the costs of healthcare have recently affected Latinos' health-seeking behaviors and their personal finances. We address this limitation through an original analysis of a unique survey of Latino registered voters. Given the current efforts to reform healthcare in the United States, an analysis of how medical costs are affecting Latinos is timely and highly informative to policymakers, particularly in light of the growing presence of Latinos in the population.

## DATA AND METHODS

The data for this analysis come from the 2009 Latino Decisions "100 Days" Survey, conducted from April 24 to May 1, 2009 (near the end of the Great Recession).[3] This survey includes 600 Latino registered voters across 19 states. Although our results cannot speak to the entire Latino population given the nature of sample, the survey is representative of the Latino voting population, as the states included in the sample account for approximately 93% of Latino voters nationwide. We believe that this is an advantage compared to other studies focused on Latinos more generally, as the registered segment of the population has the most direct impact on policy-making process through the electoral process. Furthermore, our sample of Latino citizens provides the opportunity to focus on the segment of the Latino community who will benefit from the recent federal healthcare reform efforts.

The use of a registered voter sample, however, decreases the number of respondents in our analysis who are most vulnerable to the economic consequences associated with healthcare, as Latino registered voters are citizens and of higher socioeconomic status than the non-registered population. Although a clear and important limitation, we believe that any trends established in our analysis should be considered quite compelling, as the sample allows us to analyze the relationship between the costs of healthcare and health-seeking behavior among Latinos.

Respondents had the choice to conduct the interview in either English or Spanish, with a nearly even divide between the two-language preference options—48% in English, 52% in Spanish. This survey also contains responses from Latinos from 20 different national origin populations, which allows us to explore Latino attitudes toward health policy across national origin groups, an understudied aspect of Latino public opinion polls. The data used in this analysis were weighted by nativity and gender so the sample's distribution is reflective of the overall Latino electorate.[4]

We utilize two dependent variables in our analysis, one tapping into the impact of medical bills on individual economic standing, and the other into the impact of the economic climate on health behavior. To assess the relationship between medical bill costs and personal finances, we asked respondents: *In the past 12 months, because of medical bills, have you:*

1. Used up all or most of your savings?
2. Been unable to pay for basic necessities like food, heat, or housing?
3. Had difficulty paying other bills?
4. Borrowed money or gotten a loan or another mortgage on your home?
5. Been contacted by a collection agency?
6. Declared bankruptcy?

We utilized a similar battery to examine the relationship between the current economic climate and health behavior, asking respondents: *In the past 12 months, have you or another family member living in your household [Insert Behavior] because of costs?*

1. Skipped a recommended medical test or treatment
2. Not filled a prescription for a medicine
3. Cut pills in half or skipped doses of medicine
4. Had problems getting mental health care
5. Put off or postponed getting healthcare you needed
6. Skipped dental care or checkups
7. Relied on home remedies or over-the-counter drugs instead of going to see a doctor

We re-coded these two dependent variables so that their values now range from a low of not engaging in any of the economic- or health-seeking activities, to a high of engaging in two or more of the economic- or health-seeking activities, respectively. This provides two separate dependent variables with identical values: 0 (None of the activities), 1 (One of the activities), and 2 (Two or more of the activities). This approach provides the opportunity to examine factors that contribute to the overall impact of medical bills on individual economic standing, as well as the state of the economy on health-seeking behavior.

The survey also included the opportunity to control for several important factors such as nativity, health insurance coverage, and family size; details on the measurement of these factors can be obtained from the authors. The Latino Decisions survey suited our project well due to its ability to gauge how medical costs during weak economic conditions (the Great Recession) affected Latinos' healthcare behaviors, while accounting for the relative impact of socioeconomic and demographic factors on this important phenomenon.

## ANALYSIS AND RESULTS

We begin our analysis with an overview of the average characteristics from the survey. In this exercise, we use the February 2009 Kaiser Health Tracking Poll (conducted February 3 through February 12, 2009, among a nationally representative random sample of 1,204 adults ages 18 and older) to compare the trend associated with Latinos to the general U.S. population.

Overall, Latinos felt a greater effect of medical bills upon their economic standing than the general population (see Panel A in Table 7.1). For example, 51% of Latinos had used all or most of their savings to pay their medical bills during the Great Recession, and they had been unable to pay for basic necessities like food, compared with 20% of the general U.S. population. Furthermore, 31% of Latinos had difficulty paying other bills due to medical expenses, compared to 13% of the U.S. population. Finally, another striking difference is that 15% of Latinos, but only 4% of the total population, had borrowed money or taken a loan or another mortgage on their home to cover their medical bills in 2008–09. Overall, these numbers illustrate that Latinos were under financial stress due to the high costs of healthcare during the Great Recession. It is important to note that these trends were likely higher among the general Latino population, as our sample excludes non-citizens.

This said, in some regards the impact of medical costs on health-related behavior of Latino voters mirrored that of the general population during this time (see Panel B in Table 7.1). For example, about the same percentage of Latinos in our sample and the general population reported skipping a recommended test or treatments, not filling a medical prescription, and skipping dental care due to the expense. A larger percentage of Latinos than the general population, however, reported cutting their pills in half or skipping doses of medicine (20% vs. 15%) and having problems getting medical healthcare (11% vs. 7%). At the same time, a slightly lower percentage of Latinos than adults in general reported putting off or postponing needed healthcare (25 vs. 27%) and relying on home remedies or over-the-counter drugs instead of seeing the doctor (29% vs. 35%) because of the cost.

These results point to an important outcome during the Great Recession: a significant portion of the Latino electorate (and the general population) engaged in risky health behaviors (such as skipping recommended tests or treatments or putting off or postponing needed healthcare) due

**TABLE 7.1   Impacts of Medical Bills and Costs on the Economic Standing and Health-Related Behavior of Latino Registered Voters and the General Population**

| | Latino Decisions Poll | | | Kaiser Health Tracker Poll |
| --- | --- | --- | --- | --- |
| Type of Behavior | Latinos: % Stating "Yes" | Insured Latinos: % Stating "Yes" | Uninsured Latinos: % Stating "Yes" | General Population: % Stating "Yes" |
| **Panel A: Impact of medical bills on economic standing:** | | | | |
| Used up all or most of your savings | 31% | 26% | 49% | 13% |
| Unable to pay for basic necessities (e.g., food, heat, housing) | 20% | 19% | 26% | 7% |
| Had difficulty paying other bills | 31% | 28% | 45% | 13% |
| Borrowed money or gotten a loan or another mortgage on home | 15% | 13% | 23% | 4% |
| Been contacted by a collection agency | 15% | 12% | 27% | 12% |
| Declared bankruptcy | 3% | 2% | 4% | 1% |
| **Panel B: Impact of medical costs on health-related behavior:** | | | | |
| Skipped recommended test/ treatment | 24% | 17% | 50% | 23% |
| Not filled a medical prescription | 21% | 18% | 35% | 21% |
| Cut pills in half or skipped doses | 20% | 16% | 34% | 15% |
| Had problems getting medical health care | 11% | 7% | 25% | 7% |
| Put off or postponed needed health care | 25% | 17% | 49% | 27% |
| Skipped dental care or checkups | 35% | 27% | 65% | 34% |
| Home remedies/over-the-counter drugs instead of seeing doctors | 29% | 20% | 63% | 35% |

*Source:* The "Latino Decisions" columns come from the authors' estimates using the 2009 *Latino Decisions "100 Days" Survey* (described in the text), and the "Kaiser Health Tracking Poll" is from the February 2009 *Kaiser Health Tracking Poll.*

to the overburden of medical costs. The health-seeking behavior of Latinos seems to have been altered negatively by the costs of healthcare in the United States during the economic crisis.

The results from Table 7.1 also suggest that uninsured Latinos were particularly vulnerable, as healthcare costs apparently affected both their personal finances and their health behavior. Among our sample of uninsured Latino registered voters, 49% had used up all or most of their savings, and 45% had difficulty paying other bills because of medical costs in 2008–09. A significant portion of uninsured Latinos had been unable to pay for basic necessities like food, heat, or housing (26%), borrowed money or secured a loan or another mortgage on their home (23%), or had been contacted by a collection agency (27%) due to their medical bills. Also, in response to their medical expenses, significant portions of uninsured Latinos had skipped a recommended test or treatment (50%), put off or postponed needed healthcare (49%), skipped dental care or checkups (65%), or relied on home remedies or over-the-counter drugs instead of seeing a doctor (63%). Therefore, the cost of care can lead to financial stress and risky health behavior for an already vulnerable population, namely uninsured Latinos.

Furthermore, Table 7.1 indicates that *insured* Latino registered voters were not fully protected from soaring medical costs in the Great Recession. For example, a significant portion of insured Latinos used up all or most of their savings (26%) or had difficulty paying other bills (28%) to cover their medical costs. Also, many Latinos with health insurance had failed to fill a medical prescription (18%), skipped a dental care or checkups (27%), or relied on home remedies or over-the-counter drugs instead of seeing a doctor (20%) because of the expenses.

We also examine how income affects people's health behavior and their personal finances (not shown to conserve space). It is not surprising that respondents with low income levels seem to be particularly vulnerable in terms of medical care costs. For example, 36% of Latino voters who made less than $20,000, and 38% of Latinos who made between $20,000 and $39,000, skipped a recommended medical test or treatment due to the expense. Furthermore, 42% of Latino voters with these income levels used up most or all of their savings to cover medical bills.

These data further suggest that higher-income Latino voters were not fully protected from healthcare costs either. For example, 21% of Latino voters with household incomes of $40,000–$59,000, and 14% of Latino voters earning at least 150,000 avoided a recommended medical test or treatment due to cost in 2008–09. Additionally, over a quarter of middle-income Latino voters ($40,000–59,000) as well as higher-income Latino voters ($100,000–$150,000) reported using up most or all of their savings because of medical bills. Thus, this information shows that Latino registered voters overall suffered from financial stress and could not afford basic healthcare (i.e., getting recommended tests/treatments) because of high medical costs.

The discussion above suggests that healthcare costs have had a pronounced impact on the economic status and health behavior of the Latino population. The next step in our analysis is to determine if the trends established thus far hold after we account for additional factors that can explain such behavior. This analysis will help identify which segments of the Latino population were sensitive to the cost of medical care.

We begin this discussion by investigating the impact that medical bills had on the economic standing of the Latino electorate during the Great Recession when controlling for other characteristics.[5] The results from this exercise are presented in the first two columns of Table 7.2. Socioeconomic status had a strong impact, as Latino voters with less than a high school education and those in the lowest income category (under $40,000 in household income) were more likely than other Latinos to have had multiple economic hardships resulting from the costs of medical care. Since lower income Latino voters were more likely to have economic hardships from medical bills, this placed them in a vulnerable financial position.

Moreover, household size is positively correlated with facing economic hardships due to medical care costs among Latinos. Age is also significant in this analysis, as the likelihood of facing economic hardships, such as being contacted by a collection agency to recover medical payments, was higher among younger Latino voters. This may be due to younger Latinos lacking financial planning or management skills, or being less likely to have accumulated savings to offset costs of medical care. These possibilities cannot be tested here. Also, younger people in general, not just Latinos, tend to have jobs that pay less, just due to the fact that they have been in the workforce for less time.

One of the more surprising results from Table 7.2 is that Latino voters without insurance were no more likely to have seen a negative impact on their financial status due to healthcare expenses than those with insurance, when controlling for other characteristics like household income. Having health insurance is generally perceived as a safety net to prevent significant economic hardships if and when one requires medical care. We will discuss the policy ramifications of this finding trend in more detail below.

Finally, the only cultural factor that had a significant impact on whether medical bills affect one's economic status is the preferred television language. The more English-dominant segment of the Latino voting population (measured here by an English-language preference in television-watching) was more likely to have had multiple economic hardships resulting from the costs of medical care. National origin is not significant here either, suggesting that the impact of medical bill costs is consistent across multiple segments of the Latino voting community when accounting for other socioeconomic and demographic traits.[6]

We now turn our attention to the last columns in Table 7.2, which provide results from our investigation of factors that contributed to the health-related behavioral reaction of Latinos to the costs of medical care in the Great Recession. Residing in a low-income household is again relevant, as Latino voters in households making less than $40,000 were more likely than Latinos with

**TABLE 7.2   Multivariate Analysis of the Impacts of Medical Bills and Costs on the Economic Standing and Health-Related Behavior of Latino Registered Voters**

| Characteristic | Impact of Medical Bills on Economic Standing | | Impact of Medical Costs on Health-Related Behavior | |
| --- | --- | --- | --- | --- |
| | Regression Coefficient | Odds Ratio | Regression Coefficient | Odds Ratio |
| **Demographic/socioeconomic factors:** | | | | |
| Low income (under $40,000) | 0.742*** (0.209) | 2.16 | 0.776*** (0.234) | 2.11 |
| High income ($150,000+) | −0.368 (0.324) | 0.676 | −0.665 (0.402) | 0.506 |
| Less than high school | 0.491* (0.263) | 1.53 | 0.416 (0.291) | 1.43 |
| Some college | 0.039 (0.249) | 1.04 | 0.169 (0.280) | 1.19 |
| College graduate or higher | 0.089 (0.253) | 1.09 | 0.106 (0.287) | 1.12 |
| Homeowner | 0.136 (0.194) | 1.17 | −0.065 (0.214) | 0.904 |
| Has health insurance | −0.000 (0.010) | 0.998 | 0.001 (0.014) | 1.00 |
| Age | −0.014** (0.005) | 0.984 | −0.026** (0.006) | 0.975 |
| Female | −0.127 (0.170) | 0.862 | 0.345* (0.190) | 1.38 |
| Household size | 0.121** (0.053) | 1.11 | 0.057 (0.054) | 1.05 |
| **Cultural factors:** | | | | |
| Conducted survey in Spanish | 0.263 (0.206) | 1.33 | −0.148 (0.226) | 0.854 |
| Watch primarily English television | 0.126** (0.058) | 1.14 | 0.030 (0.037) | 1.02 |
| Foreign-born | 0.004 (0.018) | 1.00 | −0.006 (0.018) | 0.994 |
| National origin | Included | | Included | |
| Impact of medical bills on economic standing | — | — | 1.56*** (0.194) | 4.86 |

***, **, * Statistically significant at the one, five, or ten percent level.

*Source:* Authors' estimates using the 2009 *Latino Decisions "100 Days" Survey* (described in the text).

*Notes:* These results are based on an ordered logit regression, where the dependent variable takes the value of 0 ("No Activities Reported"), 1 ("One Activity"), or 2 ("Two or More Activities"). The National Origin variables include Mexican American, Cuban, Puerto Rican, and Other (base); none of these variables is statistically significant at conventional levels. Contact the authors for other empirical details. The sample sizes and Pseudo R² values are 533 and 0.04 for the economic standing analysis, and 521 and 0.15 for the health-behavior analysis.

higher income to postpone or forego medical care due to the costs of these activities. This is an intuitive finding, as one would expect those with higher incomes to be able to afford medical care during economic downturns. However, the lack of significance for the high-income variable suggests similar behavioral responses to healthcare costs between middle- and high-income Latino households in 2008–09, other things the same.

This table further shows that younger Latino voters were more likely to be impacted by the costs of medical care in terms of their health-related behavior, as were Latinas. This latter finding is consistent with the apparent barriers Latinas face in accessing healthcare compared to other racial and ethnic groups (National Center for Health Statistics 2000; Ramirez and Suarez 2001). Since Latinas already tend to lack access to healthcare, it is not surprising that economic burdens disproportionately affect their health-seeking behavior. Health insurance is once again insignificant, suggesting that this resource may not be as beneficial in offsetting the rising costs of healthcare (at least for the electorate) as previously expected, after accounting for socioeconomic and demographic characteristics, such as income, gender, and age. These characteristics appear to be the driving force behind the relationship between healthcare costs and health-seeking behavior, as none of the cultural factors, including language and nativity, are significant in this model when accounting for other factors.

The bottom of Table 7.2 indicates the correlation between the two dependent variables used in this analysis. Latino voters who faced economic hardships due to medical expenses were also more likely to have responded to medical costs in terms of their health-related behavior. The robust odds ratio for this variable provides evidence of a multiplicative effect associated with medical care costs, as those who experienced a downturn in their personal financial status because of medical expenses also made tough decisions regarding their health-related activities.

## CONCLUSION

Our discussion here indicates that Latinos represent a population facing both health and economic inequalities, and are thus sensitive to healthcare costs. One third of registered Latino voters in our sample had used up all or most of their savings to cover medical expenses in 2008–09, and one quarter of them had skipped a recommended test or treatment because of the cost. These statistics are striking given that our sample excludes a particularly vulnerable segment of the Latino population, non-citizens. It is therefore likely that our findings (based on Latino registered voters) may underestimate the impact of medical costs on the economic status and health-related behavior of Latinos overall. The empirical analyses highlighted the segments of the Latino population that experienced medical costs impacting their personal finances and health-seeking behavior during the Great Recession the most—the young and those in low-income households.

We believe that one of the more interesting trends from this investigation is that health insurance did not appear to reduce the financial burdens of high medical costs as often perceived, at least among Latino registered voters, when controlling for other socioeconomic and demographic characteristics. The descriptive statistics showed that while Latinos without health insurance faced more financial and healthcare hardships due to medical costs than insured Latinos, a significant number of Latinos covered by health insurance also found themselves vulnerable to the costs of care during the Great Recession. Furthermore, our multivariate analysis indicated that when other factors such as income and education were considered, having health insurance was not a significant contributor to offsetting economic hardships or health-related behavior in response to medical expenses.

Thus, it is possible that members of the Latino electorate were under-insured during the Great Recession, such that they had to pay high out-of-pocket expenses for healthcare even when covered. This finding suggests that policies such as the Patient Protection and Affordable Care Act should address the affordability and cost of healthcare. As the new policy is scrutinized, it will be critical to assess changes in the costs of premiums, medications, and other forms of treatment to ensure that Latinos and other vulnerable populations do not face additional financial and health burdens, such as those described here. The tax credits associated with this policy will have a particular impact on the costs of care, which will likely be particular important to the Latino population in light of our discussion in this chapter. Also, since we are examining Latino voters, policymakers and politicians may wish to understand how the benefits (and costs) of the Patient Protection and Affordability Act will affect Latino voters.

Future researchers should examine how the significant costs associated with healthcare have impacted not only Latino registered voters, but also other vulnerable populations. This scholarship can assist policymakers as they attempt to expand health coverage to a wider segment of the population while reducing the costs of care at both the individual and aggregate levels. Our work here suggests that the success of federal reform should be evaluated largely on the costs of care, as providing greater access to coverage alone might not prevent vulnerable populations from facing economic hardships when they require medical care.

## NOTES

1. In this analysis we use the pan-ethnic term Latino to refer to people from Mexico, Central and South America, Puerto Rico, Cuba, the Caribbean, and any other persons from a Latino or Hispanic background.

2. Unauthorized immigrants are all foreign-born non-citizens residing in the country who are not "legal immigrants." For more on terminology see Jeffrey Passel and D'Vera Cohn (2011).
3. Registered voters were identified using the complete voter registration databases for each state and then merged with a Spanish-surname list from the U.S. Census. Phone calls were then randomly made to the phone list of registered voters. All respondents are verified to be Latino and verified to be registered voters.
4. The margin of error for the poll is +/–4%, and the response rate is 19%. The response rate was calculated based on the American Association for Public Opinion Research (AAPOR) base response rate equation. This equation provides a very conservative response rate due to essentially treating all dialed numbers as eligible participants. This is reflected in the high incidence or cooperation rate of 89% (based on AAPOR CR1).
5. We employed ordered logistic regression in the multivariate analysis for both dependent variables. Details can be obtained from the authors. Tests for collinearity among our explanatory variables were conducted with no significant inter-variable correlation detected.
6. "Other Latinos" were used as the baseline or comparison group for the analysis. It is important to note, however, that national origin variables failed to reach significance regardless of which population was used as the excluded group.

## REFERENCES

Banthin, J., Cunningham, P., Bernard, & Didem, B. (2008). Financial burden of health care, 2001–2004. *Health Affairs, 27*(1), 188–195.

Carrillo, E. J., Trevino, F. M., Betancourt, J. R., & Coustasse, A. (2001). Latino access to health care: The role of insurance, managed care, and institutional barriers. In M. Aguirre-Molina, C. W. Molina, & R. E. Zambrana (Eds.), *Health issues in the Latino community*. San Francisco: Jossey-Bass Publishing.

Derose, K. P., & Baker, D. W. (2000). Limited English proficiency and Latinos' use of physician services. *Medical Care Research and Review, 57*(1), 76–91.

Fiscell, K., Franks, P., Doescher, M. P., & Saver, B. G. (2002). Disparities in health care by race, ethnicity, and language among the insured: Findings from a national sample. In T. A. La Veist (Ed.), *Race, ethnicity, and health: A public health reader*. San Francisco: Jossey-Bass Publishing.

Fletcher, M. A. (2008, March 24). Rising health costs cut into wages: Higher fees squeeze employers, workers. *Washington Post*, pp. A01.

Hagan, J., Rodriguez, N., Capps, R., & Kabiri, N. (2003). The effects of recent welfare and immigration reforms on immigrants' access to health care. *International Migration Review, 37*(2), 444–463.

Henry J. Kaiser Family Foundation. (2008, October). Kaiser health tracking poll: Election 2008. Available at www.kff.org/kaiserpolls/upload/7832.pdf

Henry J. Kaiser Family Foundation and Health Research and Educational Trust. (2008). Employer health benefits: 2008, Summary of Findings. Available at www.kff.org.

Henry J. Kaiser Family Foundation. (2009a). Snapshots: Health care costs: Employer-based health insurance: A comparison of the availability and cost of coverage for workers in small firms and large firms." Available at www.kff.org/insurance/spashot/chcm111989.cfm

Henry J. Kaiser Family Foundation. (2009b). Health care costs, a primer: Key information on health care costs and their impact. Available at http://www.kff.org.

Himmelstein, D. U., Warren, E., Thorne, D., & Woolhandler, S. (2005, February 2). Illness and injury as contributors to bankruptcy. *Health Affairs (Millwood)*. (Web exclusive). Available at http://content.healthaffairs.org/cgi/reprint/hlthaff.w5.63v1.

Himmelstein, D. U., Warren, E., Thorne, D., & Woolhandler, S. (2009). Medical bankruptcy in the United States, 2007: Results of a national study. *The American Journal of Medicine, 122*(8), 741–746.

James, C., Thomas, M., Lillie-Blanton, M., & Garfield, R. (2007, January). Key facts: Race, ethnicity, and medical care. The Henry J. Kaiser Family Foundation.

Kullgren, J. (2003). Restrictions on undocumented immigrants' access to health services: The public health implications of welfare reform. *American Journal of Public Health, 93*(10), 1630–1633.

Leigh, W, Lillie-Blanton, M., Martinez, R. M., & Collins, K. S. (1999). Managed care in three states: Experiences of low-income African-Americans and Hispanics. *Inquiry, 36*, 318–331.

Lillie-Blanton, M., Brodi, M., Rowland, D., Altman, D., & McIntosh, M. (2000). Race, ethnicity, and the health care system: Public perceptions and experience. *Medical Care Research and Review, 57*(1), 218–235.

Mendes, E. (2012). Fewer Americans have employer-based health insurance. Gallup wellbeing. Available at: http://www.gallup.com/poll/152621/fewer-americans-employer-based-health-insurance.aspx.

National Center for Health Statistics (NCHS). (2000). *Health, United States, 2000, with Adolescent Health Chartbook*. Hyattsville, Maryland.

The National Coalition on Health Care. (2009, November 3). Available at: www.nchc.org.

Passel, J., & Cohn, D. (2011, February 1). Unauthorized immigrant population: National and state trends, 2010. Pew Hispanic Research Center. Available at: http://www.pewhispanic.org/2011/02/01/unauthorized-immigrant-population-brnational-and-state-trends-2010/.

Raiz, L. (2006). Health care poverty. *Jounal of Sociology and Welfare, 33*(4), 87–104.

Ramirez, A. G., & Suarez, L. (2001). The impact of cancer on Latino populations. In M. Aguirre-Molina, C. W. Molina, & R. E. Zambrana (Eds.), *Health issues in the Latino community*. San Francisco: Jossey-Bass Publishing.

Schoen, C., Doty, M., Collins, S., & Holmgren, A. (2005, June 14). Insured but not protected: How many adults are under-insured? *Health Affairs (Web Exclusive)*, pp. 289–302.

Schoen, C., Collins, S., Kriss, J., & Doty., M. (2008). How many are under-insured? Trends among U.S. adults. *Health Affairs, 27*(4), w298–w309.

The Office of Minority Health. (2012). Hispanic/Latino profile. Available at: http://minorityhealth.hhs.gov/templates/browse.aspx?lvl=2&lvlID=54.

Valdez, R., Giachello, A., Rodriguez-Trias, H., Gomez, P., & C. De la Rocha. (1993a). Improving access to health care in Latino communities. *Public health reports, 108*(5), 534–539.

Valdez, R., Morgenstern, H., Brown, R., Wyn, R., Wang, C., & Cumberland, W. (1993b). Insuring Latinos against the costs of illness. *The Journal of the American Medical Association, 269*(7), 889–894.

Weinack, R. M., & Kraus, N. A. (2000). Racial/Ethnic differences in children's access to care. *American Journal of Public Health, 90,* 1771–1774.

CHAPTER 8

# HISPANIC ORIGIN AND OBESITY

## Different Risk Factors, Different Responses

**Veronica Salinas**
*University of New Mexico*

**Jillian Medeiros**
*University of New Mexico*

**Melissa Binder**
*University of New Mexico*

Hispanics have higher rates of adult and childhood obesity than non-Hispanic Whites. In 2009, Hispanics were 1.2 times as likely to be obese than non-Hispanic Whites. Among Mexican American women, 73% were overweight or obese compared with 62% of the general female population. Between 2007 and 2008, Mexican American children were 1.4 times more likely to be overweight non-Hispanic White children (Office of Minority Health, 2011a).

*The Economic Status of the Hispanic Population*, pages 113–127
Copyright © 2013 by Information Age Publishing
All rights of reproduction in any form reserved.

Higher obesity rates among Hispanics are of concern because obesity is a major risk factor for diabetes, a disease that disproportionately affects the Hispanic community. Hispanics are more likely to be diagnosed with diabetes and more likely to die from diabetes compared with non-Hispanic Whites (Office of Minority Health, 2011b). Obesity is also a leading risk factor for heart disease. Mexican Americans (who represent nearly two-thirds of all Hispanics in the United States) suffer from premature death from heart disease at a higher rate than non-Hispanic Whites. Mexican American women are 1.2 times more likely to have high blood pressure than non-Hispanic White women (Office of Minority Health, 2011c). Moreover, Hispanics also disproportionately experience chronic liver disease, as both Hispanic men and women experience a chronic liver disease rate that is twice that of non-Hispanic Whites; it is also a leading cause of death for Hispanic males (Office of Minority Health, 2011d). Understanding the underlying causes and consequences of obesity among Hispanics is crucial not just because it poses a major health risk for Hispanics, but because it has implications for the health status of Americans overall, given the growing presence of Hispanics in the nation.

Previous research shows that lower exercise rates contribute to higher obesity rates among Hispanics versus other populations (e.g., Lopez-Zetina, Lee, & Friis, 2006; Carter-Pokras & Zambrana, 2001). In a study conducted in California, for example, Javier Lopez-Zetina, Howard Lee, and Robert Friis (2006) found that Hispanics had the highest median physical inactivity rates of all major racial and ethnic groups, where physical inactivity was based on self-reported exercise such as walking and bicycling. Lower rates of physical activity are also linked to socioeconomic status. Many Hispanics live in neighborhoods where it is not safe to exercise, or lack parks or places to exercise. Poverty among Hispanics means less access to facilities such as gyms and less leisure time for exercise (Perez-Escamilla & Putnik, 2007).

Furthermore, researchers have found that Hispanics have less access than non-Hispanic Whites to nutritionally adequate and safe food. Almost 20% of Hispanics are food insecure compared with 7.8% of non-Hispanic Whites. Food insecurity is not only linked to poor dietary quality and smaller food quantities, it is associated with a higher risk of obesity, particularly among low-income Hispanic women (e.g., Perez-Escamilla, Hromi-Fiedler, Vega-Lopez, Bermudez-Millian, & Segura-Perez, 2008). One reason for this may be that during times of high food insecurity, Hispanic households resort to more grain-based diets such as tortillas and rice instead of more expensive and nutritious foods such as fruits and vegetables. Also, Hispanic women may be restricting their food intake during times of food insecurity and then eating more when more food is available; this cyclical pattern of restrictive eating and overeating may contribute to obesity (Kaiser, Townsend, Melgar-Quinonez, Fujii, & Crawford, 2004).

Acculturation represents another factor correlated with the relatively high obesity rates of Hispanics. Hispanic immigrants who have been in the United States for more than 15 years are at four times greater risk of obesity and have higher body mass indices than immigrants who have been in the United States less than five years (Kaplan, Huguet, Newsom, & McFarland, 2004; Sanghavi Goel, McCarthy, Phillips, & Wee, 2004). This is attributed to Hispanic immigrants adopting less healthful dietary practices and a more sedentary lifestyle the longer they reside in the United States (Kaplan et al., 2004; Romero-Gwynn & Gwynn, 1997).

In addition to health-related outcomes, obesity can affect labor market outcomes. For example, women pay a penalty for being obese in terms of occupational attainment, but obese men are able to move into jobs that offset this penalty (Pagán & Dávila, 1997). Additionally, outward appearance can affect wage earnings, as good-looking people tend to earn higher wages than plain-looking people (Hamermesh & Biddle, 1993). Hence, health is not the only socioeconomic outcome that obesity affects.

The above discussion highlights the obesity epidemic among Hispanics and the health risks (and other socioeconomic outcomes) it poses for the Hispanic community. Since Hispanics are now the largest racial/ethnic minority group in the United States, it is imperative to understand the potential factors that contribute to obesity in the Hispanic community.

## DATA AND ANALYSIS

We use the National Health and Nutrition Examination Survey (NHANES) 2007–2008 (CDC, 2007–2008a) to examine:

1. The socioeconomic and demographic factors that contribute to obesity among adults between the ages of 20 and 64.
2. Whether these factors differ across non-Hispanic Whites, all Hispanics, Mexican Americans (the largest Hispanic subgroup), and Hispanics of other origin (referred to here as "Other Hispanics").

We focus on working-age adults because adolescent and adult obesity are generally treated separately in the literature. Additionally, elderly persons and pregnant women are usually excluded from obesity-related analyses. Because the focus of this study is to compare Hispanics with the majority non-Hispanic White population, we also exclude African Americans, Asians, and other non-Hispanic minorities. These exclusions result in a sample size of 3,066 observations for our analysis.

Body Mass Index (BMI) is calculated as weight in kilograms divided by height in meters squared. The data for BMI come from the physical examination portion of the NHANES. A person is classified as obese if his or her BMI is 30 or higher. NHANES also provides data for demographics, education, income, health insurance status, money spent on food, physical activity, and sedentary hours—characteristics which might relate to the prevalence of obesity.

Health insurance is defined here as health coverage of any kind, including private insurance obtained through an employer, or public insurance such as Medicare or Medicaid. We estimate the money spent on food per person by adding monthly household spending on food purchased at supermarkets or grocery stores, then dividing by household size. Similarly, money spent on eating out per person is calculated by adding monthly household spending on food at restaurants, fast food, school cafeterias, vending machines, and food delivered to the household, then dividing by household size.

Physical activity consists of two categories, work and leisure. NHANES (CDC, 2007–2008b) defines work as any "paid or unpaid work including gardening and household chores." Leisure is defined as any "sports, fitness, or recreational activities." Respondents are asked about two levels of physical activity, intense and moderate. Intense physical activity is defined as "causing large increases in heart rate and breathing for at least 10 min at a time." Examples include heavy work activity such as construction, digging, and carrying heavy loads and intense sports activity such as soccer, basketball, and running. Moderate physical activity is defined as "causing small increases in heart rate and breathing for at least 10 min at a time." Examples include light work activity such as gardening and household chores, and moderate sports activity such as walking, bicycling, or swimming. Physical activity hours per week are calculated by adding the total number of minutes per week spent in intense or moderate physical activity for work or leisure, then dividing by 60. This is a much more comprehensive definition of physical activity than the exercise hours measured in previous studies.

Walk/bike commute hours per week are calculated by adding the number of minutes per week spent walking or bicycling for transportation, then dividing by 60. Similarly, we estimate sedentary hours per week by dividing the total number of minutes per week spent "sitting at work, school, commuting, reading, watching television, or at a computer" by 60.

Table 8.1 shows the population characteristics by Hispanic origin. On average, consistent with other studies on ethnicity and obesity, working-age Hispanics had higher rates of obesity than non-Hispanic Whites in 2007–08: 38% of Hispanics were obese, compared with 33% of non-Hispanic Whites. The prevalence was even higher among Mexican Americans, whose obesity rate was almost 40% in 2007–08. Other notable differences include that, on average, Hispanics were younger, had lower educational attainment, and lower household income than non-Hispanic Whites. For example, 20% of

**TABLE 8.1  Obesity Rates and Other Average Characteristics of Hispanic and Non-Hispanic White Adults Ages 20–64 in 2007–2008**

| Characteristic | Non-Hispanic White | All Hispanic | Mexican American | Other Hispanic |
|---|---|---|---|---|
| Obesity | 32.9% | 38.5% | 39.8% | 36.3% |
| Body Mass Index (BMI) | 28.5 | 29.4 | 29.5 | 29.2 |
| Age (in years) | 42.2 | 37.9 | 37.5 | 38.6 |
| Female | 50.3% | 46.3% | 44.0% | 50.4% |
| Foreign born | 4.1% | 62.2% | 58.0% | 69.3% |
| Married | 67.6% | 65.9% | 67.6% | 62.8% |
| Household size | 3.0 | 4.1 | 4.2 | 4.1 |
| Less than high school | 12.4% | 44.1% | 46.6% | 39.8% |
| College degree or higher | 30.2% | 11.0% | 10.9% | 11.2% |
| Annual household income under 20,000 | 11.2% | 20.4% | 19.3% | 22.3% |
| 100,000 and over | 26.9% | 9.1% | 9.4% | 8.8% |
| No health insurance | 16.2% | 49.1% | 56.5% | 36.3% |
| Money spent on food per person per month | $160.1 | $131.6 | $125.3 | $142.4 |
| Money spent on eating out per person per month | $86.3 | $51.3 | $51.4 | $51.2 |
| Physical activity hours per week | 12.7 | 13.6 | 13.3 | 14.3 |
| Walk/bike commute hours per week | 1.6 | 2.2 | 2.3 | 2.1 |
| Sedentary hours per week | 40.8 | 29.1 | 28.9 | 29.4 |
| Sample size | 1,621 | 1,156 | 716 | 440 |

*Source:* Authors' estimates using the 2007–2008 NHANES.

Hispanics reported annual household incomes below $20,000, compared with only 11% of non-Hispanic Whites. Similarly, 11% of Hispanics held a college degree, compared with over 30% of non-Hispanic Whites. Not surprisingly, Hispanic adults were much more likely than non-Hispanic Whites to be immigrants, with 62% of Hispanics reporting a birthplace outside the United States compared with only four percent of non-Hispanic Whites.

Almost half of all Hispanics and about 16% of non-Hispanic Whites had no health insurance in 2007–08.[1] Money spent on food and eating out per person was less for Hispanics than non-Hispanic Whites, reflecting the large income differences between the groups. Finally, and in contrast with previous studies, we find that Hispanics are much less sedentary than non-Hispanic Whites. On average, Hispanics were sedentary less than 30 hr per week versus 40 hr per week for non-Hispanic Whites.

As previously mentioned, the NHANES collects much more detailed physical activity data than the exercise data reported in previous studies. The higher physical activity for Hispanics reported here may reflect occupational differences between Hispanics and non-Hispanic Whites. For example, Hispanics were more likely than non-Hispanic Whites to be employed in lower paying, manual labor jobs (i.e., more physically demanding) such as agriculture, service, mining, construction, and custodial jobs (Vega et al., 2009). As Table 8.1 shows, Hispanics were also more likely to walk or bicycle to work, school, or to go shopping. Thus, contrary to previous studies, Hispanics may actually be more active than non-Hispanic Whites when considering the physical activity involved in work, leisure, and transportation.

Since Hispanics were younger and more physically active in 2007–08, these characteristics should have decreased their risk of obesity. However, Hispanics also had lower education and income levels, characteristics which increase the risk of obesity. Another factor that may contribute to higher obesity rates is that Hispanics may *respond* differently to certain socioeconomic and demographic characteristics, compared with non-Hispanics Whites. For example, Figure 8.1 indicates that Hispanics and non-Hispanic Whites responded differently to education, where higher levels of education were associated with more obesity for Hispanics, but less obesity for non-Hispanic Whites.

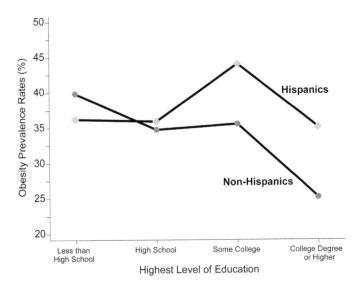

**Figure 8.1** Obesity Prevalence Rates for Hispanic and Non-Hispanic Adults in 2007-08. *Source:* Authors' estimates using the National Health and Nutrition Examination Surveys (NHANES), 2007-2008. *Note:* The sample includes 2,777 Hispanic and non-Hispanic White adults ages 20–64, excluding pregnant women.

It is therefore likely that two factors contribute to higher obesity rates among Hispanics versus non-Hispanic Whites: (a) differences in *character-istics*; and (b) differences in how Hispanics *respond* to those characteristics. If the main difference between Hispanics and non-Hispanic Whites is in characteristics (risk factors), then policy could be directed toward reducing those risk factors among Hispanics. For example, increasing educational attainment might be one avenue for reducing obesity. On the other hand, if differential responses drive the differences in obesity rates, then increases in education may inadvertently increase obesity among Hispanics. It is important that we understand whether Hispanics respond differently to develop more effective policy solutions.

To investigate this issue, we use three statistical approaches that allow us to separate characteristics and responses. For our first approach, we relate BMI and obesity to demographics (age, gender, marital status, place of birth, and household size), education, income, access to health services (measured by whether a person has health insurance), money spent on food (divided by number of household members), and physical activity (measured by reported weekly hours in (a) physical activity; (b) walking or bicycling to work; and (c) sedentary hours).[2] We first combine all Hispanics and non-Hispanic Whites together, and include Hispanic origin as an additional characteristic. In a related analysis, we separate Mexican Americans from Other Hispanics as additional characteristics. This approach helps us to determine whether Hispanics, Mexican Americans, and Other Hispanics are more or less likely to be obese than non-Hispanic Whites when we control for the observable characteristics discussed above.

Our second approach also relates BMI and obesity to observable characteristics, but we estimate the models (described in Note 2) separately for (a) non-Hispanic Whites; (b) all Hispanics; (c) Mexican Americans; and (d) Hispanics of other origin (other Hispanics). This approach allows us to compare whether the effects of observable characteristics on the likelihood of being obese vary across these groups. Our third approach uses a technique that allows us to quantify the differences in BMI between Hispanics and non-Hispanic Whites into the portion that can be explained by differences in *characteristics* and the portion that can be explained by differences in the *responses* to those characteristics.[3]

## RESULTS

Table 8.2 presents the results for our first approach where we combine Hispanics and non-Hispanic Whites. The results for BMI (shown in the first two columns) and obesity (in the second two columns) are similar. Overall, adults were more likely to be obese or had higher BMIs if they were older,

**TABLE 8.2  Multivariate Analysis of Characteristics Related to Body Mass Index and Obesity for Hispanics and Non-Hispanic Whites in 2007–2008**

| | Body Mass Index | | Obesity | |
| Characteristic | Combining Hispanics into One Group | Separating Mexican Americans & Other Hispanics | Combining Hispanics into One Group | Separating Mexican Americans & Other Hispanics |
| --- | --- | --- | --- | --- |
| All Hispanics | 1.541** | — | 0.0968* | — |
| Mexican American | — | 1.665*** | — | 0.110* |
| Other Hispanic | — | 1.310* | — | 0.0728 |
| Age | 0.0614*** | 0.0614*** | 0.00407*** | 0.00407*** |
| Female | −0.169 | −0.166 | 0.0193 | 0.0197 |
| Foreign-born | −1.080** | −1.054** | −0.0997*** | −0.0973** |
| Married | 0.632 | 0.627 | 0.0499** | 0.0495** |
| Household size | 0.276** | 0.276** | 0.0248** | 0.0248** |
| High school | −0.392 | −0.383 | −0.0427 | −0.0418 |
| Some college | −0.542 | −0.534 | −0.0200 | −0.0192 |
| College degree | −2.194*** | −2.188*** | −0.145** | −0.144** |
| Annual household (HH) income $20,000–34,999 | −0.408 | −0.415 | −0.0519 | −0.0527 |
| HH inc. $35,000–64,999 | −0.0570 | −0.0648 | −0.00184 | −0.00270 |
| HH inc. $65,000–99,999 | −0.787 | −0.797 | −0.0722 | −0.0733 |
| HH inc. $100,000+ | −1.610** | −1.620** | −0.104* | −0.105* |
| No health insurance | −0.822 | −0.844 | −0.0399 | −0.0421 |
| Money spent on food per person per month | 0.00223 | 0.00224 | 0.000144 | 0.000145 |
| Money spent on eating out per person per month | 9.79e–05 | 9.24e–05 | −4.86e–05 | −4.91e–05 |
| Physical activity hours per week | −0.00788 | −0.00778 | −0.000467 | −0.000458 |
| Walk/bike commute hours per week | −0.0201 | −0.0202 | −0.00166 | −0.00168 |
| Sedentary hours per week | 0.0405*** | 0.0405*** | 0.00161*** | 0.00161*** |
| Constant | 24.65*** | 24.65*** | — | — |

***, **, * *Statistically significant at the one, five, or ten percent level.*
*Source:* Authors' estimates using the 2007–2008 NHANES.
*Notes:* The sample includes 2,777 Hispanic and non-Hispanic White adults ages 20–64. The R2 values for the BMI results equal 0.061 for both columns. See Note 2 for more details. Please contact authors for more detailed results.

had lower levels of education and income, came from larger households, were more sedentary, and were married. Immigrants were significantly less likely to be obese and more likely to have lower BMIs. The amount of money spent on food had no effect on BMI and obesity when accounting for other characteristics.

Hispanics, Mexican Americans, and other Hispanics had significantly higher BMIs and were more likely to be obese, even with all else held equal. As seen in the first two columns of Table 8.2, compared with otherwise similar non-Hispanic Whites, BMI was 1.5 points higher for all Hispanics, 1.7 points higher for Mexican Americans, and 1.3 points higher for other Hispanics. This size of these effects is relatively large. To put this into context, a Mexican American with the same characteristics as a non-Hispanic White had a BMI that was 1.7 points higher. This means that there is a penalty just for *being* Mexican American. The size of this penalty is similar to the difference between households in the highest income category relative to those in the lowest income category. Specifically, a person in a household with income less than $20,000 had a BMI that was 1.6 points higher than a person with the same characteristics but household income of $100,000 or more.

The third and fourth columns of Table 8.2 show that the likelihood of being obese was 10 percentage points higher for Hispanics, and 11 percentage points higher for Mexican Americans, compared to non-Hispanic Whites, other things the same. Taken together, these results suggest that Hispanics, particularly Mexican Americans, were more likely to be obese and had higher BMIs than their non-Hispanic White counterparts.

For our second approach, when we run the models separately by Hispanic origin, similarities and differences between the groups emerge (results not shown to conserve space). Older and more sedentary adults in all groups, regardless of ethnic background, had higher probabilities of being obese and higher BMIs than their younger and more active peers. But for other characteristics, differences were apparent. For example, in our first approach we found that foreign-born adults were less likely to be obese and had lower BMIs than their U.S.-born counterparts. This result was driven by immigrants of Hispanic origin. BMI was 1.6 points lower and obesity risk was 12 percentage points lower for Hispanic immigrants than U.S. natives, compared with much smaller and statistically insignificant effects for foreign-born non-Hispanic Whites in 2007–08.

In terms of the relationship between education and BMI, for non-Hispanic Whites and other Hispanics with a college education, the size of the effect was nearly identical: BMI was 2.3 points lower for both groups. For Mexican Americans, however, having a college degree had a much smaller and statistically insignificant effect on BMI. And for obesity risk, non-Hispanic Whites with a college education were 17 percentage points less likely to be obese compared to people without a college degree. This means that a college education was protective against obesity for non-Hispanic Whites in 2007–08. The same did not hold true for any Hispanic group; the relationship between a college education and the probability of being obese was not statistically different from zero.

The effect of belonging to a high-income household follows a similar pattern. Non-Hispanic Whites and other Hispanics in households with incomes of $100,000 or more had lower BMIs by 1.8 points. For Mexican Americans, however, the size of the effect was less than half that much. High income did not significantly affect the odds of being obese for any Hispanic group, although it reduced these odds by 12 percentage points for non-Hispanic Whites. These results suggest that higher education and income levels were not protective against obesity for Mexican Americans, other things the same.

Altogether, the results from our first and second approaches indicate that the relationship between socioeconomic status and obesity may differ between Hispanics and non-Hispanic Whites. In the terminology used earlier, Hispanics seemed to respond differently for a given characteristic, or risk factor, than non-Hispanic Whites. We therefore use our third statistical approach (see Note 3) to quantify the relative contribution of characteristics and responses to characteristics on BMI differences between Hispanics and non-Hispanic Whites. This approach can tell us the extent to which Hispanics have higher BMIs because they have more risk factors than non-Hispanic Whites, and the extent to which higher BMIs result from different responses to those risk factors.

On average, Hispanics had a BMI of 29.4, just shy of one point higher than the 28.5 non-Hispanic White BMI. Our analysis shows that Hispanics had more protective characteristics that tended to narrow their BMI gap with non-Hispanic Whites: Hispanics were younger, more likely to be foreign-born, and were less sedentary. In fact, the effect of these characteristics on BMI outweighed those that tended to increase the Hispanic/non-Hispanic White BMI difference, including Hispanics' lower education and income levels. As such, on the basis of differences in observable characteristics, our estimates indicate that the average BMI of Hispanics should have been *less than* the BMI of non-Hispanic Whites in 2007–08.

By contrast, the Hispanic *response* to these characteristics increased the Hispanic/non-Hispanic White BMI gap by much more than the characteristics reduced it. In particular, Hispanics had lower protective responses with respect to age, physical activity, education, and income. This means that if Hispanics had the same characteristics as non-Hispanic Whites, their BMIs would be higher. We found similar results when separating Mexican Americans from other Hispanics, except that the response difference between other Hispanics and non-Hispanic Whites tended to be smaller in magnitude than the one between Mexican Americans and non-Hispanic Whites.

Our analysis tells us that most of the difference in the BMI between Hispanics and non-Hispanic Whites occurs because Hispanics (particularly Mexican Americans) respond differently to characteristics, not because of differences in the characteristics themselves. That is, the Hispanic/non-Hispanic White BMI gap is due to differences in *responses* between these two groups, not in their *characteristics*.

## DISCUSSION

Contrary to previous literature, we find that Hispanics were not less active than non-Hispanic Whites near the end of the first decade of the millennium. Unfortunately, it appears that any advantage that Hispanics may have gained with respect to reducing obesity from increased physical activity was negated by the lower protective response to physical activity compared with non-Hispanic Whites. We also find that Hispanics had a lower protective response to higher education and income levels than non-Hispanic Whites. This means that Hispanics responded differently to increased levels of physical activity, education, and income than non-Hispanic Whites. Specifically, Hispanics did not appear to benefit from these characteristics as much as non-Hispanics Whites in terms of reducing their BMIs.

We propose three possible explanations. First, the type of physical activity may contribute to the lower protective response for Hispanics. Hispanics are more likely to work in manual labor jobs (Vega et al., 2009), which tend to demand more anaerobic physical activity. These jobs may require strength and short bursts of energy but may not necessarily require aerobic physical activity. Physically demanding jobs may also induce a stress response, which may reduce the benefit from activity. If this is the case, it is possible that the type of physical activity along with the stress response induced the differential response between Hispanics and non-Hispanic Whites.

Second, in addition to being employed in more physically demanding manual labor jobs, Hispanics are more likely to walk or bicycle for transportation. This may leave Hispanics with less leisure time, thus making them more likely to engage in sedentary leisure activities such as family gatherings and visiting with friends. These social activities often include eating and drinking, which may compound the detrimental health effects of being sedentary. Although Hispanic women have been found to be less likely to engage in drinking (Carter-Pokras & Zambrana, 2001), Hispanic men may be more likely to do so. The lower protective response for physical activity may stem from the fact that we do not account for these behaviors in our model. Although Hispanics are less sedentary than non-Hispanic Whites,

Hispanics may be engaging in behaviors that lead to more severe adverse effects for the time they spend sedentary.

Third, the differential response to education and income for Hispanics may reflect a cultural difference in social networks. Mexican Americans are more likely to be integrated with family and live with or near family members than non-Hispanic Whites (Sarkisian, Gerena, & Gerstel, 2007). And while this is generally thought to have a positive effect on health outcomes, research finds that spillover and feedback effects due to social networks and neighborhood characteristics affect obesity rates (Chen, Florax, & Snyder, 2009). For example, the people that an individual surrounds him/herself with can influence eating habits. Individuals are also more likely to exercise if they live in neighborhoods that are safe, have more sidewalks, and where people exercise regularly (Chen et al., 2009). Relatively wealthy Hispanics or those who have a college education may be more likely than non-Hispanic Whites to have parents, relatives, and friends who are less educated or have lower incomes. This difference in social context could help explain the lower protective response to increased levels of income and education for Hispanics.

If this is the case, it could mean that as more Hispanics attain higher levels of education and income, these characteristics will become more protective for Hispanics. In other words, our results may merely be reflecting a lag in the response to the risk factors for Hispanics. As more Hispanics become educated and earn higher income, the risk factor response may become as protective for Hispanics as for non-Hispanic Whites. Whatever the mechanism, health policy for Hispanics must be tailored to improve risk factors as well as responses, since policy recommendations that would reduce obesity among non-Hispanic Whites may not have the same effect for Hispanics.

## CONCLUSION

As others have reported, we find that Hispanics in general, Mexican Americans, and Other Hispanics were significantly heavier on average and more likely to be obese than non-Hispanic Whites in 2007–08. Lower education and income levels among Hispanics are often proposed as explanations for their higher obesity rates. We find, however, that even after we account for age, education, income, and physical activity, all of which have strong associations with obesity risk, Hispanics had higher BMIs and were 10 percentage points more likely to be obese when compared with non-Hispanic Whites with similar characteristics.

In fact, our more detailed analysis shows that Hispanics were younger and more physically active, and that these characteristics should have decreased their risk of obesity. Instead, it appears that higher rates of obesity among Hispanics, and especially Mexican Americans, occurred because Hispanics responded differently to these characteristics than non-Hispanic Whites. In particular, Hispanics appear to have benefited less in terms of lowering their BMIs from being more physically active and less sedentary. This means that even though Hispanics are more physically active and less sedentary than non-Hispanic Whites, they still have higher BMIs and a greater likelihood of being obese. Our analysis also shows that even if Hispanics had the same levels of education and income as non-Hispanic Whites, they would still have had higher BMIs and a higher probability of being obese.

This pattern suggests that recommendations for reducing obesity, such as promoting increased activity, may benefit Hispanics less than other populations. More generally, the differential response between Hispanics and non-Hispanic Whites, and in some cases between Mexican Americans and other Hispanics, underlines the compelling need for a health research agenda that recognizes potentially large differences in public health mechanisms for Hispanics (including specific Hispanic subgroups) and other ethnic minorities, especially as these groups continue to make up an ever larger share of the U.S. population.

## NOTES

1. Jillian Medeiros and Gabriel Sanchez in chapter 7 in this volume provide a detailed discussion of explanations behind the relative lack of health insurance coverage among Hispanics (particularly in the first section of that chapter).
2. Specifically, to investigate the relationship between the observable characteristics and obesity, we employ ordinary least squares (OLS) regression analysis when using BMI as the dependent variable, and probit regression analysis when using the binary variable indicating obesity (equals one for obese individuals, and zero otherwise). Contact the authors for more details.
3. We use an Oaxaca-type decomposition analysis to estimate BMI gaps between non-Hispanics Whites and Hispanics, Mexican Americans, and other Hispanics. Contact the authors for more details.

## REFERENCES

Carter-Pokras, O., & Zambrana, R. E. (2001). Latino health status. In M. Aguirre-Molina, C. W. Molina, & R. E. Zambrana (Eds.), *Health issues in the Latino community* (pp. 23–54). San Francisco: Jossey-Bass.

Centers for Disease Control and Prevention (CDC). (2007–2008a). National Center for Health Statistics (NCHS). National health and nutrition examination survey data. Hyattsville, MD: U.S. Department of Health and Human Services, Centers for Disease Control and Prevention. Available at http://www.cdc. gov/nchs/nhanes.htm.

Centers for Disease Control and Prevention (CDC). (2007–2008b). National Center for Health Statistics (NCHS). National health and nutrition examination survey questionnaire. Hyattsville, MD: U.S. Department of Health and Human Services, Centers for Disease Control and Prevention. Available at http://www.cdc.gov/nchs/nhanes.htm.

Chen, S. E., Florax, R. J. G. M., & Snyder, S. D. (2009, July). Obesity in urban food markets: Evidence form geo-referenced micro data. Paper presented at the Agricultural & Applied Economics Association.

Hamermesh, D. S., & Biddle, J. E. (1993). Beauty and the labour market. *National Bureau of Economic Research.* Working Paper No. 4518.

Kaiser, L. L., Townsend, M. S., Melgar-Quinonez, H. R., Fujii, M. L., & Crawford, P. B. (2004). Choice of instrument influences relations between food insecurity and obesity in Latino women. *The American Journal of Clinical Nutrition, 80,* 1372–1378.

Kaplan, M. S., Huguet, N., Newsom, J. T., & McFarland, B. H. (2004). The association between length of residence and obesity among Hispanic immigrants. *American Journal of Preventive Medicine, 27*(4), 323–326.

Lopez-Zetina, J., Lee, H., & Friis, R. (2006). The link between obesity and the built environment: Evidence from an ecological analysis of obesity and vehicle miles of travel in California. *Health and Place, 12*(4), 656–664.

Office of Minority Health. (2011a). Obesity and Hispanic Americans. Available at http://minorityhealth.hhs.gov/templates/content.aspx?ID=6459.

Office of Minority Health. (2011b). Diabetes and Hispanic Americans. Available at http://www.minorityhealth.hhs.gov/templates/content.aspx?ID=3324.

Office of Minority Health. (2011c). Heart disease data/statistics. Available at http://minorityhealth.hhs.gov/templates/browse.aspx?lvl=3&lvlid=127.

Office of Minority Health. (2011d). Chronic liver disease and Hispanic Americans. Available at http://minorityhealth.hhs.gov/templates/content.aspx?ID=6207.

Pagán, J. A., & Dávila, A. (1997). Obesity, occupational attainment, and earnings. *Social Science Quarterly, 78*(3), 756–770.

Perez-Escamilla, R., Hromi-Fiedler, A., Vega-Lopez, S., Bermudez-Millian, A., & Segura-Perez, S. (2008). Impact of peer nutrition education on dietary behaviors and health outcomes among Latinos: A systematic literature review. *Journal of Nutrition Education and Behavior, 40*(4), 208–225.

Perez-Escamilla, R., & Putnik, P. (2007). The role of acculturation in nutrition, lifestyle, and incidence of type 2 diabetes among Latinos. *The Journal of Nutrition, 137*(4), 860–870.

Romero-Gwynn, E., & Gwynn, D. (1997). Dietary patterns and acculturation among Latinos of Mexican deescent. Research Report No. 23. Julian Samora Research Institute, Michigan State University.

Sanghavi Goel, M., McCarthy, E. P., Phillips, R. S., & Wee, C. C. (2004). Obesity among U.S. immigrant subgroups by duration of residence. *The Journal of the American Medical Association, 292*(23), 2860–2867.

Sarkisian, N, Gerena, M., & Gerstel, N. (2007). Extended family integration among Euro and Mexican Americans: Ethnicity, gender, and class. *Journal of Marriage and Family, 69*(1), 40–54.

Vega, W. A., Rodriguez, M. A., & Gruskin, E. (2009). Health disparities in the Latino population. *Epidemiol Review, 31*(1), 99–112.

CHAPTER 9

# MARKET WORK, HOME PRODUCTION, PERSONAL CARE AND LEISURE

## Time Allocation Trajectories of Hispanic Immigrant Couples

**Andres J. Vargas**
*Texas Tech University*

In this chapter, I analyze the patterns of time use of Hispanic immigrants and study how their allocation of time to market work, household production, personal care, and leisure change as they assimilate to the U.S. labor market. I do this analysis within a household production framework that considers the tradeoff between household and market work and the bargaining between spouses. Within this context, differences in the market wage between husband and wife relative to their marginal productivities in the household, and how these differences change as the immigrant couple assimilates into the U.S. economy, play an important role in the allocation of time within the household.

*The Economic Status of the Hispanic Population*, pages 129–140
Copyright © 2013 by Information Age Publishing
All rights of reproduction in any form reserved.

The bulk of research on the integration of immigrants to the U.S. economy has primarily focused on the labor market assimilation process and how it is determined by country of origin and the number of years since migration. Recent studies on immigrants' labor force participation consider the role of the family, mostly within a family investment framework. In this context, one member of the couple increases initially his/her labor supply in a low-paying job to allow the spouse to invest in human capital, and down the line, benefit from his or her higher earning position. This high labor force participation decreases in later years because the job he/she took upon arrival offers little opportunities for advancement. In contrast, the spouse works few hours upon arrival to allow time for human capital accumulation and gradually increases his/her position in the U.S. labor market. Alternatively, if individual investment dominates the behavior of immigrant couples, both members invest in human capital upon arrival and gradually incorporate to the labor market as their American experience accumulates.

There are no conclusive results in the empirical literature in this area. Harriet Duleep and Seth Sanders (1993) found evidence of family investment among Asian immigrant couples in the United States. Their study suggests that the rapid assimilation observed among immigrant husbands is associated with a high labor force participation of immigrant wives in the early years upon arrival to the United States. Later on, Michael Baker and Dwayne Benjamin (1997) tested the prevalence of family investment among immigrants to Canada. They attribute early low employment levels among immigrant husbands and a steady increase with years in the country as evidence of initial investment in human capital. Their wives, on the other hand, exhibit high employment levels upon arrival and a later decline relative to comparable natives. Francine Blau and her colleagues (2002) revisited the assimilation profiles of immigrants to the United States as a collective labor market decision taken between spouses. They accounted for the spouse's and own immigration history, and found evidence that disputed the earlier results in support of the family investment theory. In particular, they found that both immigrant husbands and wives, to the same degree, work less and earn less than comparable natives upon arrival to the United States, but gradually overtake comparable natives as their years since migration increase. They interpreted these findings as evidence in support of the individual investment theory.

A recent study by Daniel Hamermesh and Stephen Trejo (2012) analyzed immigrants' time use outside the family investment framework. They derived a theory of the process of assimilation based on the notion that it is costly to assimilate. Their theory predicts that immigrants will be less likely than natives to undertake assimilating activities, but conditional on undertaking them, immigrants will spend more time on them than natives. They identified education, shopping, and market work as assimilating activities and used the 2004–2008 American Time Use Survey to test the implications of their model. They reported that their theoretical predictions were supported by the data.

A substantial increase in immigrants' participation in paid employment with years in the country reduces the number of hours that they have available for other activities. Notwithstanding the large number of empirical studies on immigrants' labor market assimilation, there is little research on what happens to other activities inside the household as immigrants assimilate. Changes in the amount of time this large segment of the population devotes to non-market activities have important repercussions on their physical and economic well-being and those of their families and the areas where they live. In this chapter, I use time diary data in the American Time Use Survey (Abraham, Flood, Sobek, & Thorn, 2008) to take a deeper look into the way immigrant couples distribute their time and examine how this allocation changes as their years since migration increase. In particular, I estimate the amount of time Hispanic husbands and wives spent on market work, household production, personal care, and leisure activities, relative to comparable non-Hispanic Whites. To my knowledge, this analysis of the patterns of time use of immigrants has not been documented before in the literature.

## DATA AND DESCRIPTIVE STATISTICS

As noted above, for the purpose of this study I use the American Time Use Survey from 2003 to 2010. For the analysis, I restrict the sample to married individuals in which both members are between 16 and 64 years of age. I define Hispanic immigrants as those individuals born in Mexico, Central and South America who migrated to the United States at age 16 or older, and I use U.S.-born non-Hispanic Whites as a reference group. The sample contains a total of 14,951 non-Hispanic White native husbands, 16,524 non-Hispanic White native wives, 1,220 Hispanic immigrant husbands, and 1,386 Hispanic immigrant wives. The statistical approach basically compares the patterns of time use of Hispanic immigrants with that of U.S.-born non-Hispanic White couples. Consequently, it is important to identify the allocations of time and demographic characteristics of each of these groups.

### Daily Time Use

Panel A in Table 9.1 reports the average minutes per day husbands and wives devoted to personal care, market work, household production, and leisure activities. This table indicates that in the first decade of the new millennium, U.S.-born non-Hispanic White husbands allocated, on aver-

**TABLE 9.1  Patterns of Time Use and Socioeconomic Characteristics of Married Hispanic Immigrants and U.S.-Born Non-Hispanic Whites, by Gender, in 2003–2010**

| Characteristic | Husbands | | Wives | |
| --- | --- | --- | --- | --- |
| | Non-Hispanic White Natives | Hispanic Immigrants | Non-Hispanic White Natives | Hispanic Immigrants |
| **Panel A: Time use (minutes per day)** | | | | |
| *Personal Care* | | | | |
| Grooming | 32 | 36 | 45 | 36 |
| Sleeping | 481 | 520 | 499 | 544 |
| Eating and Drinking | 81 | 75 | 74 | 73 |
| *Market Work* | | | | |
| Working (paid-employment) | 319 | 342 | 205 | 139 |
| Commuting to work | 28 | 38 | 14 | 13 |
| *Household Production* | | | | |
| Household work | 94 | 64 | 151 | 221 |
| Care for household members | 36 | 34 | 67 | 81 |
| Purchases | 18 | 23 | 33 | 32 |
| *Leisure* | | | | |
| Socialization and relaxation | 237 | 229 | 220 | 200 |
| Sports, exercise, and rec. | 23 | 12 | 14 | 8 |
| Other activities | 90 | 69 | 118 | 91 |
| **Panel B: Demographic characteristics** | | | | |
| Age (in years) | 45.4 | 40.9 | 43.7 | 38.9 |
| Less than high school | 5.10% | 56.40% | 4.00% | 53.00% |
| High school diploma | 31.20% | 25.70% | 30.30% | 24.40% |
| Less than bachelors degree | 26.10% | 8.30% | 28.70% | 10.30% |
| Bachelors degree or higher | 37.60% | 9.60% | 37.00% | 12.30% |
| Employed | 88.20% | 91.50% | 74.10% | 47.90% |
| Unemployed | 2.90% | 5.10% | 3.00% | 7.90% |
| Non-market participant | 8.80% | 3.30% | 22.90% | 44.20% |
| Number of adults in household | 2.28 | 2.62 | 2.3 | 2.63 |
| Number of children | 0.95 | 1.62 | 0.95 | 1.6 |
| Children under 6 years old | 22.50% | 41.80% | 22.10% | 37.40% |
| Observations | 14,951 | 1,220 | 16,524 | 1,386 |

*Source:* Authors' estimates using the ATUS-X, 2003–2010.

age, 32 min to grooming, 8 hr to sleep, and 1 hr and 21 min to eating and drinking on a daily basis. In addition, they spent an average of 5 hr and 19 min working on the market and 28 min commuting. Regarding daily household production, U.S.-born non-Hispanic White husbands devoted on average 1 hr and 34 min to household work, 36 min to the primary care of household members, and 18 min to consumer purchases. This demographic group also spent 3 hr and 57 min socializing and relaxing, and 23 min in sports, exercise, and recreational activities. Their remaining time was used for other activities, such as caring for and helping non-household members; volunteering; religious and spiritual activities; professional and personal care services; household services; telephone calls, government services; and civic obligations.

Compared to non-Hispanic White native husbands, during this same time period, Hispanic immigrant males allocated an average of 36 and 33 min more to personal care and market work, in that order, per day. To compensate, they devoted 27, 20, and 22 min less to household production, leisure, and other activities, respectively. In particular, immigrant husbands spent an average of 36 min grooming, 8 hr and 40 min sleeping, and 1 hr and 15 min eating and drinking. In addition, they worked for 5 hr and 42 min and commuted for 38 min. Regarding household production, Hispanic immigrant husbands devoted 1 hr and 4 min to household work, 34 min to care for household members, and 23 min to consumer purchases. Finally, they allocated 3 hr and 49 min to socializing, relaxing and leisure; 12 min to sport, exercise, and recreation; and 1 hr and 9 min to other activities.

Regarding women, Table 9.1 indicates that non-Hispanic White native wives spent an average 45 min grooming, 8 hr and 19 min sleeping, and 1 hr and 14 min eating and drinking on a daily basis. In addition, they worked 3 hr and 25 min and commuted for 14 min. This group also allotted 2 hr and 31 min to household work, 1 hr and 7 min to care for household members, and 33 min to purchases. Concerning leisure activities, U.S.-born non-Hispanic White wives devoted 3 hr and 40 min to socialization, relaxation, and leisure; and 14 min to sports, exercise, and recreation. This group spent their remaining time on other "not classified" activities.

Relative to U.S.-born non-Hispanic White wives, in the first decade of the 2000s, foreign-born Hispanic women allocated 1 hr and 24 min more to household production and 37 additional minutes to personal care on a daily basis. To compensate, they devoted 1 hr and 8 min less to market work, 26 fewer minutes to leisure, and 27 min less to other activities. Specifically, married Hispanic immigrant women allotted 36 min to grooming, 9 hr and 4 min to sleep, and 1 hr and 13 min to eating and drinking. In addition, they worked for 2 hr and 19 min and commuted for another 13 min. Furthermore, they allotted 3 hr and 41 min to household work, 1 hr and 21 min to care for household members, and 32 min to purchases. Finally, this group spent 3 hr and 20 min socializing and relaxing, 8 min in sports, exercise and recreation, and 1 hr and 31 min in other activities.

These numbers reveal that foreign-born Hispanic couples come from countries with more traditional social norms regarding the household division of labor, in which women do most of the housework with little assistance from men, who in turn, are expected to be the main breadwinners. These observed time-use differences between Hispanic immigrant couples and non-Hispanic White natives, however, may be partly explained by their dissimilar socio-economic characteristics.

## Other Socioeconomic and Demographic Characteristics

As Panel B in Table 9.1 shows, during 2003–10, U.S.-born non-Hispanic White couples tended to be older, more educated, lived in households with fewer adults, and had fewer children than Hispanic immigrant couples. In non-Hispanic White native households, husbands were an average of 45.4 years old and wives were 1.8 years younger. Also, only 5% were high school dropouts, while 37% held a bachelor degree or higher. 88% of the husbands and 74% of the wives in these households were employed, 9% of the husbands and 23% of the wives did not participate in the labor market, and the remaining 3% of both members of the couple were unemployed. In addition, non-Hispanic White native households had on average 2.3 adults and 0.95 children, while over one-fifth had children younger than six years of age.

In Hispanic immigrant couples during this time, husbands were on average 40.9 years old and wives were 2 years younger. In addition, more than half of the respondents had not completed high school, and only 11% were college graduates. Regarding their employment status, 92% of the husbands and 48% of the wives were employed, 3% of the husbands and 44% of the wives did not participate in the market, and 5% of husbands and 8% of wives were unemployed. Finally, Hispanic immigrant households had an average of 2.6 adults and 1.6 children, and 40% had children less than six years of age.

These figures indicate that it is necessary to account for the different socioeconomic backgrounds of immigrants and non-Hispanic White natives to be able to isolate the effect of the migration history on the time allocations of foreign-born Hispanic couples.

## TIME ALLOCATION TRAJECTORIES OF HISPANIC IMMIGRANT COUPLES

In this section, I analyze the patterns of time use of Hispanic immigrant couples and examine how they changed with their years since migration while accounting for other observable characteristics. Specifically, I compare the daily allocations of time of foreign-born Hispanic husbands and wives with those of U.S.-born non-Hispanic White couples while controlling for their age, schooling level, number of adults and children in the household, the presence of children younger than six years of age, the size of their metropolitan area, family income level, and their region of residence. A detailed explanation of the estimation methodology is presented in this chapter's appendix.

## Time Use Trajectories of Husbands

Panel A in Table 9.2 shows the effects of the years since migration on the minutes per day married Hispanic immigrant men spent doing selected activities, and Panel B presents the assimilation profiles for their female counterparts. These estimates assume that both spouses belonged to the same immigration group.

These results indicate that, upon arrival to the United States, the daily time allocations of foreign-born Hispanic husbands to grooming, sleeping, eating and drinking, and consumer purchases were not statistically different from those of otherwise similar U.S.-born non-Hispanic Whites in the first decade of the 2000s. In contrast, Hispanic immigrant husbands worked and commuted 87 and 18 min more per day than native non-Hispanic White husbands, respectively. Then again, newly arrived married Hispanic men spent time on household chores and cared for household members 29 and 28 min less than their U.S.-born non-Hispanic White counterparts, in that order. While Hispanic immigrant husbands devoted an equal amount of time as non-Hispanic White natives to socialization and relaxation per day, they allocated 11 min less to sports, exercise, and recreation, and 41 min less to other activities. These estimates imply that recently arrived Hispanic immigrant husbands had relatively high labor market opportunities that made them devote less time to household production when accounting for other characteristics.

As their years since migration increased, moreover, Hispanic immigrant husbands gradually allocated more time to market work, household work, and care for household members. To compensate, they reduced the amount of time devoted to socialization and relaxation. For example, 24 years after migration foreign-born Hispanic husbands allotted 13.4 min more to grooming and eating and drinking than U.S.-born non-Hispanic White husbands, but slept for an equal amount of time. In addition, they worked on the market and commuted 98 and 17 min more than White natives, respectively. Regarding household production, the tenured Hispanic immigrant husbands devoted 23 and 20 min less to housework and care

**TABLE 9.2  Multivariate Analysis of Differences in Time Use (minutes per day) between Married Hispanic Immigrants and U.S.-Born Non-Hispanic Whites in 2003–2010**

| Difference | Years Since Migration | | | |
| --- | --- | --- | --- | --- |
| | 0 | 8 | 16 | 24 |
| **Panel A: Husbands** | | | | |
| Grooming | 1.9 | 3.9* | 5.5** | 6.7** |
| Sleeping | 21.7 | 15* | 12 | 12.8 |
| Eating and drinking | –3.2 | 3.3 | 6.6* | 6.7* |
| Working (paid-employment) | 86.8** | 77.8*** | 81.7*** | 98.4*** |
| Commuting to work | 18.1*** | 14*** | 13.6*** | 17*** |
| Household work | –29.4** | –20** | –17.9** | –22.9** |
| Care for household members | –27.8** | –28.1*** | –25.3*** | –19.2*** |
| Purchases | 6.4 | 7.8*** | 7.7** | 6.2* |
| Socialization and relaxation | –23.5 | –40.6*** | –56.1*** | –70.1*** |
| Sports, exercise, and rec. | –10.6** | –11.2*** | –12.2*** | –13.5*** |
| Other activities | –40.6*** | –21.8*** | –15.7** | –22.1** |
| **Panel B: Wives** | | | | |
| Grooming | –4.0 | 0 | 1.4 | 0.2 |
| Sleeping | 40.7*** | 32.3*** | 28.6*** | 29.5*** |
| Eating and drinking | 11.5*** | 12.4*** | 11.3*** | 8.4** |
| Working (paid-employment) | –10.8 | 25.5* | 45.2*** | 48.4*** |
| Commuting to work | –0.5 | 2.1 | 3.7** | 4.6** |
| Household work | 37.7** | 46.1*** | 53.4*** | 59.4*** |
| Care for household members | –43.8*** | –29.9*** | –20.3** | –15* |
| Purchases | 16.1*** | 5.9** | 0.1 | –1.5 |
| Socialization and relaxation | –22 | –56.7*** | –79*** | –88.7*** |
| Sports, exercise, and rec. | 0.4 | –0.7 | –1.8 | –2.7 |
| Other activities | –25.2* | –36.9*** | –42.7*** | –42.6*** |

*** , ** , * *Statistically significant at the one, five, or ten percent level.*
*Source:* Authors' estimates using the ATUS-X, 2003–2010.
*Notes:* The estimates indicate the difference between Hispanic immigrants' and non-Hispanic White natives' daily time use spend on the various activities. See the text as well as the chapter appendix for the list of control variables, along with other details.

for other household members than comparable U.S.-born non-Hispanic Whites, and allocated 6.2 min more to consumer purchases. Concerning free time activities, immigrant husbands devoted 70 min less to socialization and relaxation, and 13 min less to sports, exercise, and recreation than their U.S.-born non-Hispanic White counterparts. Finally, foreign-born Hispanic husbands living in the United States for nearly a quarter of a century assigned 22 fewer minutes to other activities than non-Hispanic White native husbands, other things the same. These figures suggest that Hispanic immigrant married men relinquished leisure time to meet work and family demands the longer they resided in the United States

## Time Use Trajectories of Wives

Turning to wives during 2003–10, Panel B in Table 9.2 shows that, upon arrival to the United States, Hispanic immigrants spent 41 min more sleeping, 11 extra minutes eating and drinking, and the same amount of time grooming as comparable non-Hispanic White natives. Time diary evidence also indicates no statistical differences between newly arrived Hispanic wives and their U.S.-born non-Hispanic White counterparts with respect to working and commuting, as well as in passive and active leisure activities. Additional estimates show that Hispanic immigrant wives devoted 44 min less to the care of household members, while they allocated 38 and 16 min more to household work and consumer purchases, respectively. Finally, foreign-born Hispanic married women new to the United States allotted 25 min less to other activities than their native non-Hispanic White counterparts. These numbers tell us that recently arrived Hispanic wives had relatively low labor market opportunities which allowed them to devote more time to personal care and household production compared to otherwise similar U.S.-born non-Hispanic White married women.

As their years since migration increased, Hispanic wives expanded their allocations of time to market work, commuting, housework, and care for household members. They accomplished this by reducing the time devoted to sleep, consumer purchases, socializing and relaxing, and other "not classified" activities. However, as their American experience accumulated, Hispanic immigrant wives held constant the time allotted to grooming, eating and drinking, and sports, exercise, and recreation. For example, 24 years after migration, Hispanic wives spent 29 min more sleeping, 8 min more eating and drinking, and the same amount of time grooming as non-Hispanic White native wives. Tenured Hispanic immigrant wives also worked on the market and commuted for 48 and 5 min more than their native counterparts, in that order. Furthermore, married female Hispanic immigrants in the United States for 24 years worked on the household 59 min more, cared for household member 15 min less, and purchased goods and services for the same amount of time as U.S.-born non-Hispanic White wives. Regarding free time, Hispanic immigrant wives allotted 89 min less to socializing, relaxing, and leisure than comparable non-Hispanic White natives, and assigned the same amount of time to sports, exercise, and recreational activities. In all, these numbers mean that as married Hispanic immigrant women assimilated into the United States, they became more productive in the household as well as in the labor market, increasing the opportunity cost of their personal care and leisure activities.

## CONCLUSION

The bulk of research on the integration of immigrants to the U.S. economy has primarily focused on the labor market assimilation process. This literature has revealed that immigrants' labor supply and wages start considerably below natives' levels, but as time allows them to accumulate skills and to assimilate to the U.S. labor market, these differences shorten. Time is finite and a dramatic increase in immigrants labor supply raises questions about the activities they sacrifice to come up with the additional hours of market work. In this chapter I took a deeper look into the way Hispanic immigrant couples in the first decade of the twenty-first century distributed their time as well as how their time allocation changed with respect to their tenure in the United States

Time diary estimates indicate that, at the time of arrival to the United States, Hispanic husbands devoted more time to market work and commuting than comparable non-Hispanic White native husbands on a daily basis, whereas Hispanic immigrant wives devoted the same time to these activities as their U.S.-born non-Hispanic White counterparts. Furthermore, married foreign-born Hispanic men devoted less time to household work at arrival than their U.S.-born non-Hispanic White counterparts, while Hispanic immigrant wives allotted considerably more time to this activity than non-Hispanic White native wives. This finding suggests that newly arrived foreign-born Hispanic husbands had higher wages or lower productivities in the household relative to those of Hispanic wives, which made them more likely to specialize in the labor market (and their wives more likely to specialize in the household sector).

The trend data show that both male and female married Hispanic immigrants increased their paid work with years since migration, but this increase was significantly more pronounced among women. A rise in the real wage with tenure in the United States appears to have drawn many Hispanic immigrant women into the market sector. Because most Hispanic men already had strong labor force participation at the time of arrival, the effect was less pronounced for them.

The findings also indicate that the increased market work was not financed by a decrease in housework or family care. In fact, Hispanic immigrant husbands and wives gradually increased their household work and time devoted to the primary care for household members as they spent more time in the United States. There is only a significant reduction in Hispanic immigrant wives' time spent on purchasing. The results further show that married foreign-born Hispanic men did not sacrifice personal care activities as they increased their market and household work, while their female counterparts reduced their sleeping and eating and drinking time. Finally, the Hispanic immigrant couples seemed to relinquish mostly passive leisure time to meet demands of family and jobs.

These trends reveal that as Hispanic immigrants assimilate into the United States, their productivity in both the household and the labor market increases, which raises the opportunity cost of time devoted to leisure and personal care, encouraging them to substitute time away from these activities and towards housework and employment. It is important to mention that even though this analysis was done for Hispanic immigrants as a whole, other studies have found significant differences in the patterns of time use, socioeconomic status, and migration patterns within the Hispanic population. A detailed analysis of the patterns of time use of Hispanic immigrants by country of origin is a topic of ongoing research, but it goes beyond the scope of this chapter.

## APPENDIX

To analyze the patterns of time use of Hispanic immigrants I estimate for each activity the following equation independently for Hispanic immigrant husbands and wives, using U.S.-born non-Hispanic Whites as the reference group:

$$Minutes_{it} = \beta' X_{it} + a_1 (Years)_{it} + a_2\ Years^2 + FIRST + SPFIRST + K_t + u_{it}. \quad (9.1)$$

For individual $i$ in year $t$, *Minutes* are the minutes spent doing a particular activity in the previous day, $X$ is a vector of control variables including age, age squared, binary variables for the highest level of schooling for both husband and wife, number of adults in the household, number of children in the household, a binary variable for the presence of children younger than six years, indicators for the size of the metropolitan area, family income level, and four regional indicators. The assimilation profile with respect to the immigrant's own time in the United States is captured by the variable years since migration (*Years*), which equals 0 for natives. Following Blau, Kahn, Moriarty, & Souza (2002), I calculated the years since migration variables by evaluating the categorical period of immigration variables at the midpoints of the indicated intervals and used the year of interview minus 1950 for the open-ended category before 1950. The variables *FIRST* and *SPFIRST* are indicators for first generation immigrants for the respondent and the spouse, respectively. Finally, $K$ is a vector of common year effects, and $u$ is an error term assumed to be normally distributed.

In Equation (1), immigrants and natives are combined. The equation allows each spouse's immigration history to influence the time use behavior of both spouses. I do not include cohort-of-arrival effects in the regression because there are only eight years of data in the sample, and becuase arrival cohorts can only be defined in five year intervals. In addition, I do not include in the model the years since migration of the spouse because they are highly correlated with the years since migration of the respondent and will introduce a problem of multicolinearity. I estimate Equation (1) using ordinary least squares because it produces unbiased estimates in a time-diary context, even though a large fraction of observations might have values of zero for the time spent in a particular activity. For more details, including the regression results, contact the author.

## REFERENCES

Abraham, K. G., Flood, S. M., Sobek, M., & Thorn, B. (2008). *American time use survey data extract system: Version 1.0* [Machine-readable database]. Maryland Population Research Center, University of Maryland, College Park, Maryland, & Minnesota Population Center, University of Minnesota, Minneapolis, Minnesota.

Baker, M., & Benjamin, D. (1997). The role of the family in immigrants' labor-market activity: An evaluation of alternative explanations. *American Economic Review, 87*(4), 705–727.

Blau, F. D., Kahn, L. M., Moriarty J. Y., & Souza, A. P. (2002). The role of the family in immigrants' labor-market activity: Evidence from the United States. National Bureau of Economic Research Working Paper 9051.

Duleep, H., & Sanders, S. (1993). The decision to work by married immigrant women. *Industrial & Labor Relations Review, 46*(4), 677–690.

Hamermesh, D., & Trejo, S. (2012). How do immigrants spend time? The process of assimilation. *Journal of Population Economics,* Published Online 01 September 2012. doi:10.007/s00148-012-0440-x.

CHAPTER 10

# LESSONS LEARNED AND ISSUES RAISED ABOUT HISPANIC ECONOMIC OUTCOMES

**Alberto Dávila**
*The University of Texas–Pan American*

**Marie T. Mora**
*The University of Texas–Pan American*

Throughout this book, the growing presence of the Hispanic American population has been highlighted along with the challenges this ethnic group has faced over the last several years and might continue to face in the future. Given that Hispanics currently represent one out of every six Americans, understanding their economic status is arguably of greater interest to social scientists and policymakers than in the recent past.

## HUMAN CAPITAL

In Chapter one, we showed that Hispanics as a group have become a rising economic force in the country. Indeed, in the first decade of the new

*The Economic Status of the Hispanic Population*, pages 141–148
Copyright © 2013 by Information Age Publishing
All rights of reproduction in any form reserved.

millennium, the rapid growth of the Hispanic population in the United States, in addition to other socioeconomic-related issues discussed in this book, manifested itself through the prism of this group's purchasing-power status. The chapter points nonetheless to this potential being hindered by Hispanics' low education levels compared to those of non-Hispanics. But, it hints of optimism on this front as Hispanics appeared to have gained some ground with respect to their educational attainment and other socioeconomic outcomes in the first decade of the 2000s.

With regards to Hispanic educational achievement, Mark López in Chapter two presents a paradox. Despite low education levels, Hispanics seem to place a large value on education. The survey used in this chapter's analysis suggests an explanation: Hispanics value education and might wish to attain higher levels of this important human capital factor, but they are constrained by economic family obligations. The chapter further reveals Hispanic youth as being optimistic because they view a brighter financial future than that of their parents. What remains to be seen is whether this level of optimism has been tempered by the detrimental labor-market consequences of the Great Recession. As noted in that chapter, in the fourth quarter of 2007, the unemployment rate among 25-to-34 year old Hispanic college graduates was 2.9% and after the Great Recession, by 2010, it stood at 8.1%. Equally of note, the deterioration in the labor-market position of young educated Hispanics worsened during this time compared to their non-Hispanic White counterparts, but the Hispanic young without these education credentials fared even worse.

Chapter three's study by Arturo Gonzalez on the English-language literacy gap between Hispanics and non-Hispanic Whites, and particularly the analysis of the intergenerational narrowing of this gap, provides further policy insights into ways to promote the human capital base of the growing Hispanic population. He suggests that through investments in enhancing English-language literacy rates among the Hispanic population, the educational and intellectual achievement for parents and their children would increase. Gonzalez notes that these gains should advance this group's college enrollment and graduation rates, and promote better programs at schools as well as in-home benefits, such as reading for leisure. This chapter posits that while failure to implement such policies is unlikely to stunt further gains in literacy for Hispanics in both absolute and relative terms, implementing such policies may speed up their assimilation process with respect to English-language literacy.

The findings from these first three chapters yield related issues about the future significance of Hispanic human capital to policy and social science. For example, consider the education quality differential between Hispanics and non-Hispanic Whites. Would education equality between these two groups bring about earnings parity between them? It could be argued that

Hispanics would still earn less than non-Hispanic Whites because, as we noted in Chapter one, education obtained abroad tends to pay less in U.S. labor markets than schooling acquired in the United States (e.g., Trejo, 2003). Moreover, even among Hispanics who attend U.S. schools, if educational stratification provides them with lower education quality than non-Hispanic Whites, this would probably also be reflected in lower wages. Perhaps, differences in schooling quality help explain Gonzalez's finding in Chapter three that third-plus generation Hispanics have lower English-language literacy rates than their non-Hispanic White counterparts, despite attending U.S. schools.

Another issue to consider is the extent to which self-reporting influences these changing human capital differentials. In a 2009 Pew Hispanic Center Report, Jeffrey Passel and Paul Taylor make the point that, at the end of the day, it is the individual who decides to report his/her Hispanicity. Brian Duncan and Stephen Trejo (2011), moreover, have raised the question of self-reporting and Hispanic identity. They argue that as individuals are farther removed from their Hispanic roots, they become less likely to self-identify as being Hispanic. If so, assessing changing gaps in human capital characteristics between Hispanics and non-Hispanic Whites might prove to be a difficult endeavor.

In addition, intermarriage rates might continue to blur the Hispanic/non-Hispanic identification, making the aforementioned distinctions increasingly problematic. For example, Wendy Wang in a 2012 Pew Social & Demographic Trends report shows that among the newly married, intermarriage was 15% in 2010 compared to 6.7% in 1980 in the United States. This rate was higher for Hispanics, with over one quarter (26%) reporting intermarriage.

The differences in human-capital characteristics between Hispanic and non-Hispanic Whites might also be masking larger differences between Hispanic subgroups and non-Hispanic Whites. As the first three chapters discuss, Hispanic immigrants tend to have less education, lower levels of English-language fluency, and as highlighted in Chapter three, lower rates of English-language literacy, than their native counterparts. Moreover, heterogeneity exists across the specific national-origin Hispanic populations. What these chapters do not consider is that even *within* a specific Hispanic subgroup, considerable differences in human capital might exist along other demographic dimensions, such as phenotype. Sociologists such as Edward Telles (2004) and, more recently, Andrés Villarreal (2010) have found that in Latin America (Brazil and Mexico, respectively), darker individuals are stratified into occupations with lower prestige and have lower levels of education and economic standing than their fairer counterparts. It follows that immigrants might import these social stratification structures when they migrate to the United States (e.g., Dávila, Mora, & Stockly, 2011).

## POVERTY

The next set of chapters delves into issues of Hispanic poverty. Mary Lopez finds that employment, particularly full-year/full-time, has a larger effect in magnitude than schooling on the likelihood of being impoverished. An important issue to consider is why Hispanics who work full-time still have higher poverty rates than non-Hispanic Whites. From a policy perspective, she notes that efforts to reduce poverty among Hispanics (and other populations) should not only address ways to improve their educational attainment and labor market outcomes, but should include other policies that aim to improve the English-language proficiency and child-care for single mothers.

Lopez also notes that it is important to ask whether these poverty outcomes are endogenous to Hispanics or whether they are an outcome influenced by exogenous actions by the non-Hispanic White majority, as Carlos Siordia and Ruben Farias suggest in Chapter five. Siordia and Farias assume that individual-level prejudices by non-Hispanic Whites coalesce to influence the formation majority bias against Hispanics. If so, however, a relevant point to make regarding Siordia and Faria's analysis is whether these purported discrimination tendencies are permanent effects, or if they are short-lived, as Becker's discrimination theory predicts. That is, if there is a cost to discrimination that is borne by the discriminating group, over time and under competitive circumstances, discriminating employers should be driven out of the market. Beyond economic reasons, we have already noted that these seeming exogenous discriminatory practices might dwindle over time because of rising Hispanic exogamy rates and a decline in the self-reported Hispanicization in the United States.

Refugio Rochín in Chapter six notes, as do Sordia and Farias for Hispancs in urban areas, the potential inverse relationship between Hispanic spatial concentration and this group's lower earnings in the rural United States. Both the Rochín and the Sordia/Farias studies attribute this association to the theoretical proposition that non-Hispanic Whites' discrimination-taste intensifies against Hispanics as the latter group becomes more visible. Aside from the sustainability of this type of labor-market discrimination mentioned above, these assessments beg the following question: at which point does the population reach a tipping point where the majority/minority distinction is blurred? The most obvious case is that of Puerto Rico. Moreover, in four states, non-Hispanic Whites represent less than half of the population (New Mexico, Hawaii, Texas, and California), and in about a dozen metropolitan areas on the U.S. mainland, Hispanics represent over half of the residents. In fact, Hispanics account for over nine out of ten residents in two: Laredo, Texas (with a 95% Hispanic share among all adults ages 25–64 in 2010), and McAllen, Texas (with a 91% adult Hispanic share).

The presence of Hispanics in an area and their lower earnings there might also be rooted in endogenous decisions made by this group about location choice. To be closer to the Hispanic culture and fellow ethnics, Hispanics might be willing to accept a lower "compensating wage" as workers attempt to maximize their utility and not their earnings. Arguably, Hispanic workers (particularly those who are relatively mobile) can select the level of labor-market discrimination they are willing to endure by choosing the area where they work. Perhaps the growing geographic dispersion of Hispanics into "non-traditional" areas might be partly reflective of these endogenous labor market choices.

With regards to the rural sector, Rochín's discussion that the sector has lost U.S.-born labor has also been reported in studies such as that of Micha Gisser and Alberto Dávila (1998). According to Gisser and Dávila, over the past several decades, there was a positive self-selection of rural labor with high observed and unobserved characteristics to the urban sector, a sector that has relatively high rewards for these characteristics. Therefore, the non-Hispanic "White flight" from the rural sector observed by Rochín in Chapter six could also be explained by these economic forces. Indeed, it could be argued that the Hispanic immigrant influx into the rural sector that Rochín reports could be seen as a means to replenish the sector's outflow of high quality non-Hispanic White labor.

A final point to be made about studies presented here (and generally) dealing with poverty issues is that the federal poverty thresholds are difficult to assess in a practical manner. To be sure, assessing them has important policy implications, particularly in terms of public finances and efficient resource allocation. Still, these types of studies could go further by considering how inter-regional cost-of-living differences also distort the identification of impoverished populations. For example, according to salary.com in late 2010, the cost of living in Los Angeles was 91.5% higher than that in McAllen, Texas—an area identified as one of the poorest in the United States and one in which Hispanics represent over nine of ten residents.

Consider that a two-person family with an income of $14,366 (the poverty threshold) in McAllen had the same purchasing power as $27,509 in Los Angeles at that time. Two-person families in Los Angeles with a $25,000 income were not considered impoverished, and therefore would have been ineligible for many public aid programs. Yet, they were worse off in real terms than some families technically identified as poor residing in low-cost areas like McAllen. Therefore, national poverty thresholds overstate poverty rates among residents of low-cost areas, and understate them for high-cost areas. It would be of interest if future studies provided estimates of how this "mismeasurement" affects the observed impoverishment rates of Hispanic versus non-Hispanic populations.

## HEALTH AND HEALTH-RELATED BEHAVIOR

Inequalities do not end with education, earnings, and poverty. They continue with respect to health insurance coverage and health-related behavior. Jillian Medeiros and Gabriel Sanchez in Chapter seven, and Veronica Salinas, Jillian Medeiros, and Melissa Binder in Chapter eight suggest that Hispanics face different health-related constraints than non-Hispanic Whites, even when controlling for other socioeconomic characteristics. The Medeiros and Sanchez study is of policy concern because it reports that, at least among registered Hispanic voters, this demographic group faces relatively high financial constraints regarding paying for medical care.

With regards to the Medeiros and Sanchez chapter, however, the behavioral aspects related to Hispanics and the costs of medical services might be of interest in exploring these issues. For example, what role do families play, in both time and financial resources, vis-à-vis the treatment of illnesses? What is the level of trust that Hispanics have for health providers (as the literature has shown differences in the trust that Hispanics show for other services, such as in the banking industry)? To what extent does this group have an expectation that its healthcare needs will be eventually treated abroad (in the case of Mexican Americans, in Mexico, particularly those who live in border cities)? And, if these types of behavioral differences are found between Hispanics and non-Hispanic Whites, will they dissipate in future generations?

The Salinas, Medeiros and Binder study specifically points to one of the root causes of Hispanic health issues: this ethnic group's relatively high obesity propensity even after controlling for differences in education and other observable features. On the one hand, we have reported here reasons to be optimistic about the educational progress of Hispanics. On the other, the Salinas, Medeiros and Binder results suggest that education gains might not be the panacea for Hispanic obesity-related health concerns. They find that while a college education led to lower obesity rates for non-Hispanic Whites, this was not necessarily the case for Hispanics. They do note, however, that their results may not hold in the future as this ethnic group becomes increasingly economically and *culturally* assimilated to the pan-ethnic groups representing the U.S. non-Hispanic White population. Indeed, this possibility echoes our discussion above regarding the changing patterns in self-identity and exogamy rates for Hispanics.

But what if Hispanics assimilate economically but not culturally? The Salinas, Medeiros and Binder findings, coupled with Andres Vargas' study in Chapter nine on the time usage of married Hispanic immigrants vis-à-vis non-Hispanic Whites, suggests that these health differentials might be exacerbated as populations integrate. However, whereas the Vargas' results suggest that recreational physical activity is lower (and worsens with time) for Hispanic immigrant men, Salinas, Medeiros and Binder show that when further considering physical activities associated with non-recreation (such as being employed in more physically demanding manual labor jobs, and walking or bicycling to work), Hispanics appear to be more physically active than non-Hispanic Whites. Consider that as the education levels of Hispanics improve, this ethnic group's presence among professional and more sedentary jobs would probably increase (as might their propensity to drive instead of walk to work), thus reducing their overall physical activities if other time-usage patterns remain the same. In this case, there would be reasons for growing policy concerns on how to address the health disparities between Hispanics and other U.S. populations.

To be sure, the relationship between assimilation and Hispanic health is more complex than it would appear. Numerous studies have shown that the longer immigrants reside in the United States, the less healthy they become. Also, U.S.-born Hispanics tend to be more overweight than immigrants, as reported by Salinas, Medeiros, and Binder. And Vargas shows Hispanic immigrants are assimilating with respect to time-use, as he notes that the longer they reside in the United States, their productivity in both the household and the labor market increases; this raises their opportunity cost of time devoted to leisure and personal care.

## CONCLUSION

The chapters in this volume highlight that Hispanic Americans lag behind non-Hispanic Whites with respect to various economic outcomes. Education, immigration, and English-language fluency appear to be major factors in explaining their relatively low socioeconomic status. However, the latter two issues might not play as large of a role in the near future as they do today. Consider that a 2008 Pew Hispanic Center report by Jeffrey Passel and D'Vera Cohn projects that the future growth of the Hispanic population in the United States will be driven more by U.S. births than immigration, such that by 2045–50, the number of Hispanic U.S. births will be double the number of new immigrants. These changes mean that a rising share of the Hispanic population will grow up in the United States, learn English at a young age, and attend U.S. schools. It follows that issues related to education, such as school retention and schooling *quality*, might become an increasingly important component to the economic success of Hispanic Americans.

But, will school quality be a Hispanic American issue or a broader issue for Americans in general? As the next generation of young Hispanics goes through its life cycle, will it assimilate into the pan-ethnic non-Hispanic White culture or, instead, will these populations *converge* into an evolving American culture which has many elements of Hispanic cultures? Already, the non-Hispanic White majority has adopted Hispanic-origin foods and many Spanish idioms into their daily lives. This type of convergence, along with growing intermarriage patterns, might make some of our current policy designs that aim to enhance Hispanic economic outcomes moot. In their place, issues such as those investigated by Villarreal and more recently by Dávila, Mora, and Stockly dealing with *mestizaje* (the spectrum of European vs. indigenous features of an individual) faced in countries such as Mexico, and more broadly in terms of skin shade as suggested by Telles in Brazil, might be more relevant.

As we note in this book, there are states and other geographic areas were the Hispanic American population outnumbers non-Hispanic Whites. We venture that research into the dynamics of these areas, as they pertain to the issues addressed in this book (and of, course, others pertaining to the intersections of these) might yield important insights into what the future will bring for Hispanics and more broadly, for the socioeconomic and political environment of the nation.

## REFERENCES

Dávila, A., Mora, M. T., & Stockly, S. K. (2011). Does mestizaje matter in the U.S.? Economic stratification of Mexican immigrants. *American Economic Review, 101*(3), 593–597.

Duncan, B., & Trejo, S. (2011). Tracking intergenerational progress for immigrant groups: The problem of ethnic attrition. *American Economic Review, 101*(3), 603–608.

Gisser, M., & Dávila, A. (1998). Do farm workers earn less? An analysis of the farm labor problem. *American Journal of Agricultural Economics, 80*(4), 669–682.

Passel, J. S., & Cohn, D. (2008, February 11). *U.S. population projections: 2005–2050.* Washington, DC: Pew Hispanic Center, www.pewhispanic.org.

Telles, E. E. (2004). *Race in another America: The significance of skin color in Brazil.* Princeton: Princeton University Press.

Trejo, S. J. (2003). Intergenerational progress of Mexican-origin workers in the U.S. labor market. *Journal of Human Resources, 38*(3), 467–489.

Villarreal, A. (2010). Stratification by skin color in contemporary Mexico. *American Sociological Review, 75*(5), 652–678.

Wang, W. (2012, February 16). *The rise of intermarriage: Rates, characteristics vary by race and gender.* Washington, DC: Pew Social & Demographic Trends, www.pewsocialtrends.org.

# APPENDIX

---

# MAJOR DATASETS USED

## AMERICAN COMMUNITY SURVEY (ACS)

The American Community Survey (ACS), a random nationally representative sample of the U.S. population, has been conducted annually by the U.S. Census Bureau since 2000. In addition to basic demographic characteristics, these data contain detailed individual-level information (such as earnings, occupations, education, employment, and so forth) as well as household-level information (such as family income and whether this income fell below the federal poverty thresholds). These data can be downloaded free-of-charge from the University of Minnesota Population Research Center at www.ipums.org through the Integrated Public Use Microdata Series (IPUMS); see Steven Ruggles and his colleagues (2011) for more information. Since 2005, the annual datasets have included approximately one-percent of the U.S. population; sampling weights are included to preserve the national representation of the data. ACS data can also be obtained in three-year clusters (e.g., 2006–2008), which contain approximately three-percent of the U.S. population.

## AMERICAN TIME USE SURVEY (ATUS)

The American Time Use Survey (ATUS), an ongoing time diary study, is funded by the U.S. Bureau of Labor Statistics (BLS) and fielded by the U.S. Census Bureau. The nationally representative ATUS contains individuals

*The Economic Status of the Hispanic Population*, pages 149–151
Copyright © 2013 by Information Age Publishing
All rights of reproduction in any form reserved.

ages 15 or older, randomly selected from a subset of households that completed their participation in the Current Population Survey (CPS). In addition to demographic variables, the ATUS includes detailed information on the specific time individuals spent in more than 400 activities during a 24-hr period. These data can be downloaded free-of-charge through the American Time Use Survey Data Extract System (ATUS-X) at www.atusdata. org; see Katharine Abraham and her colleagues (2011) for more information. Approximately 20,000 ATUS interviews were completed in 2003, and 14,000 interviews have been completed per year since then.

## NATIONAL ASSESSMENT OF ADULT LITERACY (NAAL)

The 2003 National Assessment of Adult Literacy (NAAL), sponsored by the National Center for Education Statistics (NCES), is a nationally representative assessment of English-language literacy among American adults age 16 and older. Over 19,000 adults participated in the 2003 assessments (1,200 of whom were inmates in federal and state prisons interviewed in 2004). In addition to the literacy assessment scores, demographic and socioeconomic characteristics are included. More information about the NAAL, including accessing the data, can be obtained from the NCES (2012).

## NATIONAL HEALTH AND NUTRITION EXAMINATION SURVEY (NHANES)

The National Health and Nutrition Examination Survey (NHANES), a major program of the National Center for Health Statistics (NCHS), is part of the Centers for Disease Control and Prevention (CDC). The NHANES examines a nationally representative sample of about 5,000 persons each year. It has an interview component (which includes demographic, socioeconomic, dietary, and health-related information) and a physical examination component (which consists of medical, dental, and physiological measurements, plus laboratory tests administered by highly trained medical personnel). For more information on these data, including data access, see the CDC (2012).

## PUBLIC USE MICRODATA SAMPLE (PUMS) FROM THE 2000 DECENNIAL CENSUS

The Public Use Microdata Sample (PUMS) from the 2000 decennial census is a nationally representative sample based on the long-form census questionnaire administered to one of every six households. The one-percent PUMS, provided in the IPUMS (see the ACS summary above), contains approximately one percent of the U.S. population in 2000. As with the ACS, the PUMS contains detailed individual- and household-level information. In fact, the ACS questionnaires are based on the 2000 long-form census questionnaire.

## REFERENCES

Abraham, K. G., Flood, S. M., Sobek, M., & Thorn, B. (2011). *American Time Use Survey Data Extract System: Version 2.4* [Machine-readable database]. College Park: Maryland Population Research Center, University of Maryland; and Minneapolis: Minnesota Population Center, University of Minnesota; www.atusdata.org.

Center for Disease Control and Prevention. (2012). National Center for Health Statistics (NCHS). *National Health and Nutrition Examination Survey Questionnaire.* Hyattsville, MD: U.S. Department of Health and Human Services, Centers for Disease Control and Prevention; http://www.cdc.gov/nchs/nhanes.htm.

National Center for Education Statistics. (2012). *National Assessment of Adult Literacy (NAAL): A Nationally Representative and Continuing Assessment of English Language Literary Skills of American Adults.* Washington, DC: Institute of Education Sciences, www.nces.ed.gov/naal/.

Ruggles, S. J., Alexander, T., Genadek, K., Goeken, R., Schroeder, M. B., & Sobek, M. (2011). *Integrated Public Use Microdata Series: Version 5.0* [Machine-readable database]. Minneapolis: Minnesota Population Center, University of Minnesota; www.ipums.org.

# ABOUT THE EDITORS

**Marie T. Mora**, is Professor of Economics at The University of Texas—Pan American (UTPA). Prior to joining UTPA in 2002, she was a tenured faculty member at New Mexico State University. Professor Mora earned her PhD in economics from Texas A&M University, and BA and MA degrees (also in economics) from the University of New Mexico (UNM) in her hometown of Albuquerque. She has also been a Visiting Scholar at the National Poverty Center at the University of Michigan (February 2010), as well as at the Robert Wood Johnson Foundation (RWJF) Center for Health Policy at UNM (March-April 2010).

Professor Mora's research interests are in labor economics, particularly in the areas of Hispanic labor-market outcomes (including self-employment), the economics of the U.S.-Mexico border, and the economics of education. She has published over 30 refereed journal articles on these topics in the past 15 years, including in *Industrial Relations, American Economic Review, International Migration Review, Economic Development and Cultural Change, Social Science Quarterly, Economics of Education Review*, among others. She just completed co-authoring a book (with Alberto Dávila), *Hispanic Entrepreneurs in the 2000s* in production at Stanford University Press, and her first co-authored/co-edited book, *Labor Market Issues along the U.S.-Mexico Border*, was published by the University of Arizona Press in late 2009.

In terms of her professional service, Professor Mora has been a Member of the American Economic Association's Committee on the Status of Minority Groups in the Economics Profession since 2008 (a committee which she chaired in 2011). She is also serving on the Data Users Advisory Committee for the U.S. Bureau of Labor Statistics, the Editorial Board of *Social Science*

*The Economic Status of the Hispanic Population*, pages 153–154
Copyright © 2013 by Information Age Publishing
All rights of reproduction in any form reserved.

*Quarterly*, and the Board of the American Society of Hispanic Economists. Moreover, Professor Mora was previously a Mentor in the Diversity Initiative for Tenure in Economics (DITE) Program, and she served two consecutive two-year terms as President of the American Society of Hispanic Economists (October 2006–September 2010).

**Alberto Dávila**, is currently Professor of Economics and V.F. "Doc" and Gertrude Neuhaus Chair for Entrepreneurship at The University of Texas—Pan American. He is also serving as Department Chair for the Department of Economics and Finance, a position he has held since January 1997. Before joining UTPA in 1996, Professor Dávila was a tenured faculty member at the University of New Mexico, and his first professional employment was as an Economist at the Federal Reserve Bank of Dallas. Professor Dávila earned his PhD in Economics from Iowa State University in 1982, with his doctoral dissertation focusing on U.S.-Mexico border wage differentials. He also has an MS degree in economics from Iowa State University, and a BA degree in economics from The University of Texas—Pan American.

Professor Dávila's research interests include the economics of the U.S.-Mexico border, the economics of immigration, and Hispanic labor markets (including entrepreneurship). He has been publishing on border-related topics since 1982, first appearing in the *Federal Reserve Bank of Dallas' Economic Review*. His work has also appeared in such journals as *Economic Development and Cultural Change, American Economic Review, Economic Inquiry, Journal of Regional Science, American Journal of Agricultural Economics, Industrial Relations, Journal of Population Economics, Public Choice, International Migration Review,* among others. Professor Dávila just finished writing a book (co-authored with Marie T. Mora), *Hispanic Entrepreneurs in the 2000s,* in production at Stanford University Press, and his first co-authored/co-edited book, Labor Market Issues along the U.S.-Mexico Border, was published by the University of Arizona Press in late 2009.

Professor Dávila has received such professional honors as the Small Business Administration District Research Advocate Award for the Lower Rio Grande Valley (2003), and the Distinguished Alumnus award from the College of Business Administration at U.T.-Pan American's 75th Anniversary (Fall 2002), among others. He has also served as a Mentor in the Diversity Initiative for Tenure in Economics (DITE) Program.

CPSIA information can be obtained
at www.ICGtesting.com
Printed in the USA
LVHW081533100122
708185LV00004B/211